MODERN CHRISTIAN REVOLUTIONARIES SERIES

General Editor:

DONALD ATTWATER

BISHOP GRUNDTVIG:
A PROPHET OF THE NORTH

He who praises a man ought to follow him, and if he be not ready to follow him he ought not to praise him.—*St. John Chrysostom*

MODERN CHRISTIAN REVOLUTIONARIES

BISHOP GRUNDTVIG: A PROPHET OF THE NORTH

By
E. L. ALLEN, M.A., Ph.D., D.D.
Lecturer in Theology at the University of Durham

His day was the greatest the Northland has seen.—*Björnson*

WIPF & STOCK · Eugene, Oregon

Wipf and Stock Publishers
199 W 8th Ave, Suite 3
Eugene, OR 97401

Bishop Grundtvig
A Prophet of the North
By Allen, E. L.
Copyright©1949 James Clarke Lutterworth Press
ISBN 13: 978-1-5326-9326-7
Publication date 6/4/2019
Previously published by James Clark & Co., LTD., 1949

CONTENTS

I.	PREPARATION	9
II.	CONFLICT	19
III.	FULFILMENT	29
IV.	ODIN AND CHRIST	39
V.	CHURCH AND PEOPLE	54
VI.	THE LIVING WORD	62
VII.	EDUCATION FOR LIFE	77

LITERATURE

Begtrup, Lund, and Manniche: *The Folk High-schools of Denmark* (1926)

Campbell O.: *The Danish Folk School* (1928)

Davies: *Education for Life: A Danish Pioneer* (1931)

Davies: *Grundtvig of Denmark: A Guide to Small Nations* (1944)

Manniche: *Denmark: A Social Laboratory* (1939)

The author wishes to express his special indebtedness to Lehmann, *Grundtvig* (German translation with biographical introduction by Ammundsen, 1932), and also to the Rev. A. M. Sensen for criticisms and suggestions.

1

Preparation

THE history of Denmark during the nineteenth century, seen from one point of view, is a sad spectacle of descent from greatness to comparative insignificance. In the year 1800 Denmark ranked among the colonial powers, her merchant navy sailed the seven seas and had augmented considerably its share in the world's carrying-trade while Great Britain was engaged in war with her American colonists, and in the Napoleonic wars her fleet was a prize for which to contend. In the year 1900 Denmark saw herself overshadowed by the military power of her German neighbour and safe only as she was content to take her place among the small nations and contract out of the power-politics of the Continent. At the beginning of the century the Danish king ruled also over Norway and Schleswig-Holstein: the loss of this meant the reduction of his territory to a mere fragment of what it had formerly been. A series of disasters marked the passage of the years: Denmark shared in the defeat of Napoleon and lost territory to Sweden as a consequence, while she was the first victim of Bismarck's policy of aggrandizement.

But the same story might be written with at least equal truth in wholly different language, telling how a people came into possession of its soul through suffering and gave the world an object-lesson in true greatness. The Denmark of 1900 could boast a virile and independent peasant class, enjoying the prosperity which its genius for co-operation had earned and capable of political responsibility. A state had come into existence which deliberately subordinated external to internal policy and concentrated its energies on the welfare of the people, and which as a result exercised no small measure of moral leadership. And this result had been achieved not so much in spite, as because, of the set-backs and misfortunes of the century. The loss of Schleswig-Holstein and the threat to agriculture from the development of the grain-producing areas of the New World might have disheartened another people; they only stimulated the Danes to fresh and more vigorous effort.

The scheme of reforestation and land-reclamation which was carried through in the second half of the century with such great success might well serve as a symbol of the whole movement of which it was one part. Time was when 'the heather waved in lone sovereignty over one-seventh of Denmark's surface' and the sands were swept for miles inland before the wind; ingenuity, skill and perseverance combined to turn more than 2,500 of these lost acres into forest or tilled land. So the Danish people carried on a vast work of spiritual reclamation by which they gained inwardly what they had lost outwardly.

But whence did Denmark obtain the resources which enabled her to accept defeat in battle and pass on from it to bold enterprises of freedom, justice, and ordered progress? In part, no doubt, the forces which worked for recovery had already been liberated before the peril began. In the last two decades of the eighteenth century, on the initiative of the more far-seeing among the great landowners, agrarian reforms were introduced which abolished all that remained of serfdom, established the peasant in security upon the soil, and removed restraints on trade. On the eve of the French Revolution, therefore, those social changes had been effected peaceably in Denmark which were impossible in many other countries without violent upheaval. Nevertheless this is by no means the whole story: the liberation of the peasantry was only the beginning, and their intellectual and spiritual awakening in the nineteenth century were still to come. To this one man contributed beyond all others, and the dynamic, prophetic personality of Grundtvig ranks among the nation-builders of all time.

§

Nicolai Frederik Severin Grundtvig was born on the 8th September 1783 in the manse at Udby in southern Sealand where his father was parish minister. For generations his mother's family as well as his father's had given its sons to the service of the Church. He grew up amid quiet country surroundings, now astir with the new life which the liberal agrarian policy of Reventlow had brought to the peasantry. In after years he contrasted the wisdom with which Denmark handled her agricultural problem and the wholesale sacrifice of the rural population which disgraced the corresponding period in English history. His mother was the principal influence upon him in those early days, though he tells us also of his debt to an old, crippled woman about the house. From his mother he derived his poetic genius, his love for the old Norse sagas, and that Lutheran piety which even in the Age of Reason lingered on in such out-of-the-way places as the Udby manse. What better preparation for his life-work could have been found than this, to grow up amid country scenes and country folk, nourished on the simple piety of the family, finding delight in the Church's hymn-book and in the festivals of the Christian year?

It was assumed, of course, both by the parents and by the lad himself that he would take up his father's calling. With that in mind, he was sent away from home for six years of private tuition in another manse, this time in Jutland, and then to the grammar school at Aarhus for two years. This was the period during which the map of Europe was torn up and then redrawn, first by the armies of the French Revolution and then by those of Napoleon. Grundtvig spent them in what he was afterwards to describe as 'a school of death', a hateful place in which successive generations of Danish youth were drilled to a harsh system and surrendered their originality to an alien culture. To judge from his own account, he paid no attention whatever to his studies and he had scarcely a good word later for any of his teachers. But he left for the university with an excellent report and his classical scholarship was adequate to the needs of the translator and the historian in after years, while he never lost his enthusiasm for the Greek language and the Greek contribution to civilization.

But there was nothing at the grammar school to continue what he had acquired in his childhood years at home and there was nothing when he went in 1800 to the university at Copenhagen. His later judgement on his theological course was that he found no Christianity in it and that, of course, when he sat his examination at the end there was none in his papers! But we shall see that Grundtvig was a man disposed to harsh judgements of those who for any reason displeased him, and we have to bear in mind that he did not actually attend the lectures of any of the professors whom he criticized so bitterly. The rationalism of the eighteenth century was still in the ascendancy in intellectual circles, though a generation of students was arriving at the university for whom what was taught there was as the offer of a stone to a man seeking bread.

One event, however, at the outset of these student years was sufficiently dramatic to disturb the apathy of anyone who was living in the capital. Denmark was one of the powers which combined to form the Armed-neutrality League during the struggle between Great Britain and France, and the former country retaliated by despatching Nelson with a fleet to attack Copenhagen. The gallant but unsuccessful resistance which the capital offered served to rouse the national spirit of the people and to unite against the enemy the various elements which owned allegiance to the Danish crown. We know that Grundtvig drilled with the student volunteer corps which was raised for the defence of the capital, but he seems to have been unaffected by the experience. Indeed, the extracts from his diary which have been published suggest a singularly stale and barren existence. Even when he returned home for the Christmas vacation and went into the pulpit, he had nothing better to offer the congregation than moral platitudes. What surprises one even more is that apparently his parents were well satisfied with the sorry performance of their son.

But new life was already beginning to stir in Copenhagen. The Age of Reason was passing and the Romantic movement was beginning to make its influence felt in the northern lands. This was of such importance for the future development of Grundtvig that we must digress for a moment to offer some account of it. The Romantic movement was at the same time a reaction against the ruling ideas of the previous century and a development of them. The critical philosophy of Kant showed how reason itself could lead to the apprehension of a world beyond that of the mere intellect, and if Kant was indebted to pietism and rationalism, he was also profoundly influenced by Rousseau. Typical of the new tendency is Schleiermacher's vindication of religion by locating it in the realm of feeling, as against the attempts to reduce it to a set of ideas or a series of moral obligations. Inevitably, such an understanding of religion led to something very like pantheism, as also to emphasis on aesthetic values more than ethical. The new vocabulary made use of such terms as 'creative', 'genius', 'holy', 'divine', and what the eighteenth century had dismissed as 'enthusiasm' was now brought back to honour. Schelling restored the lost sense of the unity of man and nature and gave a poetical interpretation of the latter which was to supersede the scientific. History came into its own again and men showed a capacity to enter sympathetically into the life of past generations, as in the novels of Sir Walter Scott. There was a cult of personality, freedom, and self-expression which sometimes degenerated into mere lawlessness, but which sought in fact to substitute an inner law for the harshness of an outward constraint. There was a hunger to live and not merely to know.

The influence of Schleiermacher upon Danish theology at the time was practically negligible, but there were others who have to be taken into account in any estimate of what was at work in the minds of the young men who were Grundtvig's companions. For Fichte an intense moral conviction was the starting-point of his thinking; the world exists only as the sphere of exercise and duty for the human self. It arises by action, and for action conscience is the supreme legislative authority, and the individual finds his satisfaction and fulfilment in the service of the moral order to which he belongs. This is the theme of *The Vocation of Man*, a summons to ethical heroism which appealed to the finest spirits of the time, and which found a ready response when reproduced in the exuberant, berserker English of Carlyle. Grundtvig remained to the end of his days a man who had been stirred to the depths by Fichte.

The philosophy of Schelling was introduced to Denmark while he was at the university and by his cousin on the mother's side, Henrik Steffens, who had sat at the feet of the master himself and whose lecture-room was now crowded with eager young men waiting for the world of liberation. The German thinker rejected the mathematical explanation of nature which the eighteenth century had carried to triumph and saw nature instead as a pulsing, throbbing life. The lower forms of being are not hostile to spirit but akin to it and so many efforts after it. There is a unity in all that we break up and dissect, our analysis falsifies the divine and perfect whole. Spirit and Nature, Infinite and Finite are but differing aspects of the One.

With these presuppositions, world-history is seen as the continuous self-expression of the Godhead, in which each nation and each epoch has its place assigned to it; it is a divine work which never ceases and which we are called to continue by our own activity. The artist is the man to whom the vision of unity is convincingly clear and who is able, by the forms in which he clothes it, to communicate it to his fellows; he is priest of the Godhead and teacher of mankind.

Posterity has perhaps done less than justice to Schelling, principally because he was so soon overshadowed by the greater genius of Hegel. It is not difficult, however, to see wherein lay the appeal of these two men: they provided a standpoint from which it was possible to survey as a unity the various territories of our experience and they gave their hearers the sense of belonging to a mighty whole. The lectures of Steffens kindled a fire in more than one young and seeking soul, but it was not until later that Grundtvig drew from them what they had to give. His awakening was to come in another way, after he had completed his theological course and left the university.

§

There were others in those days who after training for the ministry were indisposed to accept it as their vocation. Fichte and Kierkegaard are numbered among these: the latter had private means which enabled him to assert his independence, but the others were not so fortunately situated. But it was usually possible for a young theologian, not yet ordained, to secure a post as private tutor in some well-to-do family and Grundtvig found such an opening. He was engaged in this way by a landowner on the small island of Langeland. He was twenty-two years of age, and the son of a country minister found himself introduced into a new social environment. The mistress of the house, Constance Leth, was six years older than himself. From the moment of their first encounter she made a deep impression upon him and closer relationships left him passionately in love with her. They read together *The Arabian Nights* and sometimes she would sing to him in the evening. Self-possessed, frank and open-hearted as she was, she gave the young tutor her friendship and only found out afterwards that it was more than he could stand.

An intense inner conflict ensued as he strove to bring his passion under control. He loved her—yes, but she was the wife of another and therefore he must not love her. He was able to conquer his passion, summoning to his aid all his native moral earnestness. Other salutary influences were not wanting to his hour of trial—the half-forgotten Lutheranism of childhood's years, the heroic legends of his people with their joy in conflict and their crown of praise for the successful warrior, and last but not least the trumpet-call of Fichte's idealism. He emerged from the ordeal a conqueror and enriched in soul by what he had endured: indeed, if any single event was more the making of this man than the others which entered into his life, it was his love for Constance Leth and his victory over it.

In three ways the new Grundtvig was disciplined by what he went through and made ready for his life-work. In the first place, his erotic experience did for him what it did for many others in those days, it opened in his soul the springs of poetry. His whole emotional life was released at last, the ice of rationalism broke and the warm streams of feeling and imagination began to flow. His boyhood's love for nature came back to him and in the plow driven across the fields he saw a symbol of his own lot: so must he be torn by suffering that God's seed might be sown in him and grow up one day to a rich harvest.

In the second place, he saw a new and deeper meaning

in the old legends of gods and giants which were the heritage of his people. His *Mythology of the North* (1808) brought him a reputation not only among his own countrymen but in the other Scandinavian countries and in Germany. At this stage he was able to combine the two allegiances, to Odin and to Christ, to the sword of the one and the cross of the other, for were not both alike children of the All-Father?

§

The third result of what happened in Langeland deserves fuller treatment. It was his conversion. In 1808 he left for Copenhagen, there to continue his researches in Norse mythology. His father was growing old and wished him to return to Udby as his assistant; but he was not at first disposed to comply, nor did the authorities favour the suggestion. But he took the steps necessary for ordination and the circumstances connected with this, as will be described in the next chapter, brought him into conflict with the authorities and aggravated his inner conflict. He fell into a depressed and melancholy condition; the struggle against his own sexual nature had virtually exhausted him. In the middle of December what he called 'the hammerstroke' fell upon him. As he read the fiftieth psalm in the Bible which Constance Leth herself had presented to him, he saw himself as a sinner and under God's condemnation. In thought, if not in act, he was an adulterer; his heart was empty and cold; he could stand in the pulpit and preach, but it seemed as though he had never actually known God. And the best in him was a monstrous pride: he had thought himself called to the defence of Christianity and all the while he was only Christ's in name; he had striven against temptation, but in his own strength. Under the strain of self-reproach and yearning he broke down utterly. Friends undertook to see him back to his father's house, and one of them relates that when they stayed at a wayside inn for a night, he found Grundtvig on his knees, crying out that the devil had wound himself around his body like a great snake.

It was Christmas when he arrived home and the old memories returned, bringing healing with them. He saw where his sin lay: it was the sin of arrogance. He had lived hitherto in pride of reason and pride of will, seeking to order his own life and more heathen than Christian. But in the church of his childhood's days he found peace; Christ spoke to him out of the hymn-book he had loved as a boy, Christ met him in forgiveness at the altar. In return, he surrendered himself; he would accept his vocation without reserve and stand henceforth at his Lord's disposal.

Shortly before Whitsunday of the following year he was ordained and returned to Udby as assistant to his father.

2

Conflict

'ONE must have chaos in one to give birth to a star.' Nietzsche's words might well serve as a motto for the life of Grundtvig. His was an intense, prophetic nature, akin at once to the heroes of his country's legendary past and to the bards who sang of them. He was creative because he was open to conflict and therefore to growth, many-sided, defying all efforts to bring him under a simple formula. Scholar and singer, dreamer and man of action, he lived at the point at which Denmark's present distresses were illuminated and relieved by her grandiose past. His mind was of the intuitive and not of the discursive type; he saw the truth in a flash and did not arrive at it by a course of argument. And what he saw was so clear to him that he could not imagine how anyone else could miss it; therefore he was apt to condemn out of hand those who did not share his visions and were sceptical in face of his enthusiasms. He worked by assertion, throwing out his challenge to all and sundry, as one invested with some kind of authority.

There was, of course, something pathological in his make-up and on more than one occasion he was the victim of a mental breakdown. The last instance was of a peculiarly disconcerting character. He was then 83 years of age when one Sunday from the pulpit he began to address the Queen-Mother as the Queen of Sheba who had come to hear the wisdom of Solomon, and went on to declare that a greater than Solomon was present. It was the break-through in an extravagant form of that sense of mission which was an integral part of his personality. But, apart from such unfortunate mischances, he was liable alternately to fits of deep depression and moods of exultation. He was essentially an inspired man, one who worked by the help of forces beyond himself, and while the inspiration was with him he had the energy and the strength of a viking; after it had left him, he would be listless and weak. These alternations can be traced in all his work, which at times soars to heights of imagination and power which would entitle him to a place among the greatest, and at times sinks to the level of platitude or runs to waste in some desert of obscure verbiage.

Being such a man as this, he was inclined to hasty action and lacked consideration for the feeling of others. It was easy for him to identify his own judgement with the truth of God and to denounce his critics as God's enemies. He could indulge in sweeping condemnation of an author whom he had never read, just as in later years he could denounce wholesale men from whom he had at the time learned much. Even his closest friends had occasion to complain of his suspicion and mistrust. He acted on impulse and seemed to love conflict for its own sake: at any rate, in the period of his life upon which we have now entered we shall see him more than once engaged in quite unreasoning controversy and thus seriously injuring his own career.

His defects, however, were those of the prophet and it is with men like the prophets of Israel or with their counterparts in later day, such as Savonarola and John Knox, that he finds a place. And the Denmark which shared in the defeat of Napoleon needed a prophet. In 1807, afraid of Napoleon's intentions, the British demanded the surrender of the Danish fleet and when this was refused they invested the capital by land and sea. This time Grundtvig shared the popular enthusiasm for resistance, but a three-days' bombardment left the government with no alternative to submission. As a sequel, Denmark declared war upon Great Britain and thus found herself involved seriously when Napoleon's fortunes began to decline, especially as Bernadotte, now crown prince of Sweden, used every opportunity to press hard upon the neighbouring kingdom. The state went bankrupt and by the humiliating peace of 1814 Norway was transferred to Sweden as reward for Bernadotte's abandonment of his former master—an event which led to vigorous denunciations of Swedish perfidy by Grundtvig.

Already he had won a reputation as a controversialist, first by the poem *The Masked Ball* (1808), in which he scourged the frivolity of the capital amid the national peril, and next by a sermon which he preached in 1810 as part of his examination for ordination and admission to a charge. In this he cried shame upon the rationalistic spirit which, as he declared, still pervaded the state church, falsifying the plain witness of the Bible and making Christianity of no effect. His examiners were well satisfied with the sermon, though one of them, very naturally, took the opportunity to recommend a milder treatment of his colleagues in the ministry for the future. But it was typical of his hasty and impulsive nature that he printed the sermon and thus increased the offence a hundredfold. One immediate result was a formal protest from the clergy of the capital and the demand that the rash preacher should at least be censured by the university authorities. This, no doubt, was one of the factors which contributed to the breakdown later in the same year. Eventually, however, the storm blew over: he was cautioned appropriately enough but there was no inclination to penalize him by interfering with his career.

On October 9th of the same year he entered into one of those brief periods of excitement and heightened self-consciousness which were characteristic of him: this too was of the elements which went to make up the inner conflict of that time. He was reading Kotzbue's *History of Prussia* and came to the depreciatory expression 'the barren cross'. He flung the book from him in a sudden burst of indignation and sprang up. It was at that moment as if a power from beyond himself laid hold of him; he too was called to be a crusader and a reformer, bringing to honour that same cross of which a man could speak so lightly. The mood of tense enthusiasm lasted several days. As we have seen, before long he was humbled by the realization of how utterly unfitted he was for such a work. And even when he confessed before God his sin of pride and found peace of mind, he was not wholly delivered. Pride remained with him to life's end, that pride which is the besetting temptation of the man who knows that God has chosen him as his instrument.

§

In January 1813 his father died and Grundtvig was released from his duties as assistant at Udby: he therefore moved to Copenhagen to give himself to literary work. In seven years he was able to accomplish an incredible amount of work, including the translation into Danish of the Anglo-Saxon *Song of Beowulf* and the Latin *Chronicle* of Saxo Grammaticus. In 1821, now a married man and the father of a family, he left the capital for a country living, only to return in the following year to Copenhagen. It is strange that he who spent most of his life in the city was to influence it so little; born among the rural population, he was to find among them chiefly a response to his appeal.

By this time new forces were at work in the religious life of the capital and of the nation. Groups of earnest folk were being gathered together for self-examination and devotion, as revival broke out, and two movements which were to leave their mark permanently on the Danish Church belong to this period. In 1814 a Bible society was formed and in 1821 the Danish Missionary Society. But there was nothing here which attracted Grundtvig; his conversion had been not only to Christ, but also to a flaming, even a fanatical, orthodoxy and he was in the mood for controversy.

In one of his poems, he enumerates the sources on which he drew for the new life which came to him at the time of his spiritual awakening. He describes himself as a man on the edge of an abyss, seeking deliverance and finding it in the presence of God everywhere, in the poet's song, in the wisdom of the wise, in the march of events across time, in the mythology of his people, but above all in the Bible, and only there at last with full certainty. It was as a Bible-Christian that Grundtvig began to preach in Copenhagen, as one for whom the Bible was inspired in every word and possessed of an unquestioned authority. He spoke of it during this period as Christ's representative on earth, as his Body, and he could even—quite erroneously, of course—appeal to Luther as his forerunner in this unquestioning acceptance of the letter of Scripture.

His first passage of arms was with the scientist Örsted: there was an exchange of pamphlets in which Grundtvig cannot be said to have got the better of his opponent, who rightly reproached him with making an illegitimate appeal to the authority of the Bible. On the next occasion, he tried to raise the students of the theological faculty against one of their professors and so secure his dismissal because he dared to question certain parts of the Bible. The professor in question was urged to bring a libel action against the attacker, but declined to do so. Grundtvig's next opponent was not so generous.

He was Professor Henrik Nicolai Clausen, a man who has for his own merits a sure place in the history of the Danish Church during the ninteenth century. Born in 1793, he was called in 1821 to the New-Testament chair at Copenhagen and later combined with these duties the teaching of systematic theology. His father had been the protagonist of rationalism in his day and as such had had occasion to criticize Grundtvig for his trial-sermon of 1810. The son studied under Schleiermacher at Berlin and learned from him that it was possible to combine reverence for the Church's tradition with a scientific attitude towards the Bible. The rationalism which he had inherited from his father was thus modified by an element of liberalism. A few years after his entry upon his professorial duties, he published his book on *Catholicism and Protestantism*, in which he spoke somewhat disparagingly of Luther, questioned the authority of the Bible, and left a place for reason in Christian theology.

Characteristically, Grundtvig bestowed no great attention on the contents of the book before replying to it: he can only have glanced through it in cursory fashion when he rushed into print with a furious attack upon the author. It was a battle of Thor against the giants and he brandished his hammer vigorously before bringing it down on his luckless opponent. In *The Church's Answer* he branded him as one who despised and ridiculed the word of God, declared him unfit to hold his teaching office, and summoned him, in the name of the Church, either to recant his errors or to resign.

Clausen did not submit passively to such an onslaught: he also had weapons at his disposal and did not hesitate to wield them. He instituted a libel action against Grundtvig, and even those who differed theologically from him yet felt that he had just cause to be offended. But the legal process proved a dilatory one and threw Grundtvig again into a state of inner conflict, so that he contemplated withdrawal from public activity. He had little zest for the practical side of the care of a congregation and his preaching had not evoked the response for which he hoped. He was therefore in the mood for resignation.

The opportunity was not long in coming. In 1826, the year after his attack on Clausen, Denmark was to celebrate a thousand years of Christianity. As the festival drew near, Grundtvig prepared to make his contribution to the celebrations by the composition of several appropriate hymns.

Naturally enough, he wished these to be sung by his own congregation and gave notice of the proposal through the newspaper. That, however, was to introduce unauthorized elements into the service and the authorities took action: as the person immediately responsible for such oversight was Clausen's father, he had a personal, as well as an official, reason for the prohibition. Grundtvig's answer was to resign his charge.

He was not altogether without financial resources, as he was in receipt of a grant from the king for his historical studies. Wealthy friends were also ready to come to his assistance, and one of them proposed that he should use his leisure to collect and edit the hymns of the Danish Church, at the same time enriching them with new hymns from his own pen. Meanwhile, the action against him remained unsettled, and when it was concluded, his difficulties were only increased thereby. For he was adjudged guilty and required to pay compensation to Clausen, while any future work of his was to be subject to censorship. One can well imagine that this last penalty was by far the most serious one for so independent a spirit as his.

§

At this juncture, fortunately, assistance came to Grundtvig from the highest quarter in the land. He enjoyed the patronage of King Frederick VI and when the latter asked him one day what he proposed to do now that he had resigned from his congregation, he answered, on the impulse of the moment, that he had no plans and had not the slightest idea what he would do, unless, to be sure, the king would send him to England to study the Anglo-Saxon manuscripts there. The king granted his request, and between 1829 and 1831 he was three times in England. The journeys and the new experiences which they brought with them were among the most fruitful events of his life, and when he took up again his public activities it was as a man matured in spirit and ready to throw himself into the tasks of contemporary life.

Yet the visits to England (the last in 1843) must not be thought of as undertaken with any such end in view: he who was to be a prophet of life to his people had come across the seas in quest of ancient manuscripts primarily. He visited the libraries of London, Cambridge, Oxford, and Exeter, improving his knowledge of Anglo-Saxon, collating manuscripts and projecting a series of publications which was eventually to be undertaken by someone else. He met some of the leading figures of the day, including Pusey and Newman: but high-churchman though he was, he found nothing in the Tractarian movement to appeal to him. He went to Edinburgh and met Chalmers, but again with little or nothing in the way of mutual understanding as a result of their encounter. If he condemned the church life of the day as wanting in vitality and could say that Anglicanism had no adequate sense of the Church's importance and regarded the sacraments merely as external symbols, we can only explain this as we remember that Grundtvig, in such matters, did not regard knowledge as necessary before he passed judgement.

In two respects, however, his experiences in England were determinative for his whole future. He came back with a consciousness of having been introduced to a new and most attractive style of life, one which combined personal liberty with fidelity to tradition. The roots of English society were still in the middle ages, a native culture had been preserved in a land less exposed than his own to the vicissitudes of history, the institutions and the literature of the people were reminiscent of the past and continuous with it. Yet there was a freedom in the air which was lacking in a Denmark where the principle of absolute monarchy was as yet unchallenged. England, as it seemed to him, had been able to achieve that synthesis of social solidarity and individual liberty which is the best guarantee of national health.

In the second place, in the colleges of Oxford and Cambridge he met a type of education which contrasted favourably with the formalism under which he had suffered alike at the grammar school and the university. The colleges with their historical associations and their beautiful setting amid river, lawn, and garden, the close personal relationship between tutor and student, the survival into modern times of the medieval conception of a university as something much more than a collection of lecture-halls, as in fact a common life spent in the quest for knowledge—how he longed to find some means by which he could bring these within reach of his own people! No doubt he idealized the educational system of England and did not realize how restricted was the circle of those who enjoyed the privileges of the older universities; nevertheless, he had now something positive to oppose to the 'school of death' which he remembered with such bitterness.

It must not be overlooked, of course, that the new thoughts which appear in the third and final phase of his development were already present in germ with him before he crossed the sea to England. His experiences there served as a fresh stimulus, they gave him confidence in ideas which had begun already to arise in his mind, and they enabled him to bring to unity the various tendencies of his personality. Hitherto he had been a party-leader in the church, he was now to become a national figure. His vocation, he saw, was a larger and bolder one than he had hitherto imagined: God had called him to act and not merely to speak, he was to enter into the difficulties and problems which beset his country and to bring to it fresh sources of hope and confidence. He had known himself called to quicken life in individuals through word and song, now he perceived that he must take part in shaping those institutions within which his people lived. With the watchword 'Freedom' on his lips he entered the phase of maturity and fulfilment. In the language of the ancient sagas he called for 'Freedom for Loki, freedom for Thor', or borrowing the words of the Lord, he who had once been so insistent to root out the tares in the Church's field now demanded for them the same right to growth as for the wheat. He was as sure as ever that truth is sacred, but he had learned that it is also mighty and can afford to tolerate error, for against error it will at last prevail.

3

Fulfilment

THE little country of Denmark, having been deprived of Norway in 1814 as the penalty of a mistaken attachment to the cause of Napoleon, might have lived thereafter in peace had it not long before given hostages to fortune through the ambiguous connection of Schleswig and Holstein with the monarchy. When Duke Adolphus of Holstein died in 1490, the nobility of the two duchies elected Christian I, king of Denmark, as their lord on condition that the union between the two duchies should remain unquestioned. The establishment in 1815 of the German Confederation created a problem, as the population was not homogeneous in the two districts. Holstein was clearly German, while Schleswig was Danish in the north and German in the south; at the same time, local patriotism was strong and the two duchies wished to remain together. Frederick VI of Denmark, as duke of Holstein, took that area into the federation, but kept Schleswig out of it as distinctively Danish. Into the criss-cross of political dispute which followed we need not enter: a situation had arisen which seemed to be beyond the wit of man to deal with.

With the accession of Christian VIII to the throne of Denmark in 1839, the problem became more acute than ever. A separatist movement in the two duchies evoked as a reaction a "Greater Denmark" agitation for the annexation of Schleswig. It was at this juncture that Grundtvig came forward as a leader with a programme, equally opposed to any surrender of any essential Danish claims and any expansion of the country at the expense of another nationality. The frontier of Denmark, he urged, should be carried no farther south than the Danish language and the Danish spirit had already gone. Once, perhaps, the whole of Schleswig had been Danish in this true sense, but the southern half was now German in its cultural allegiance and must be allowed to continue so. What was to be feared and to be prevented was the germanization of the Danish stock in the northern half of the duchy. The spiritual integrity and unity of the Danish people must be preserved. And the means to that was the school.

In the years since his return from England he had employed both the written and the spoken word in advocacy of a new conception of education, an education for life instead of for death, an education based on the Danish language, history and tradition, instead of either Latin or German. In such a school formal lectures would be avoided and the influence most relied on would be that of teacher upon student, the enthusiasm of the one kindling the enthusiasm of the other. He secured the sympathy of the king and his consort and even projected a People's University, as one might call it, under royal patronage at Soro.

These hopes were not to be realized, but the impending struggle with Germany forced into other channels the energies which Grundtvig had aroused. His ideals were carried out on a larger scale than he had anticipated, though after a different pattern. In answer to his summons to a spiritual warfare, a group of patriotic Danes in Schleswig came forward with the funds to build a school at Rodding on the frontier of Denmark and Schleswig. The enterprise was inaugurated by Grundtvig himself, when he addressed a massed assembly of ten thousand and announced that the school was to be built as a bulwark to protect Denmark and her people against the invasion of an alien culture. Some sentences from the prospectus issued by the school are worth quoting:

'The object we have set ourselves is to found an institution where peasant or citizen can secure knowledge and skill for use and pleasure, not so much with respect to his particular livelihood and business as to his part as a son of the country and a citizen of the state. . . . We call it a High School because it is not to be the usual boys' school but an institution of learning partly for young men after confirmation age and partly for older youths and men, and we call it a Folk High School because members of every station of life are admitted although it is especially suited to peasants and it is from them that most of the pupils are expected.'

While Grundtvig accepted the school at Rodding as a weapon in the struggle against Germany, he did not regard it as in any sense fulfilling his educational ideals. The teachers were themselves men with an academic training and they employed just those formal methods of instruction with which he wished to break. The new venture which he advocated was not really made until Denmark's security had been shaken in the war of 1848 and the duchies had been taken from her in that of 1864.

Frederick VII came to the throne in 1848: he took over from his father and promulgated as almost his first public act a constitution which was intended at once to unite Denmark and the duchies and to confer upon them a common parliament. The scheme satisfied no one, and a monster petition to the king, presented by a procession of ten thousand citizens to the palace, put such pressure upon him that the scheme was abandoned and a Greater-Denmark ministry was formed. The people of Holstein replied by rebellion, and Prussian and North-German troops entered the duchy in its support. The result was inconclusive, but in 1852, by the Treaty of London, agreement was reached between Denmark and the foreign powers interested and the union of the two duchies with the Danish monarchy continued.

1848 was also the year of revolutions throughout Europe, and in the midst of the war Frederick VII convened a national assembly to draw up a constitution. Grundtvig was elected to this and thereafter to the diet which it brought into existence, though he did not attach himself to any of the parties. In the first half of his career he had been a supporter of the absolutist principle, in part, no doubt, because of the friendly attitude of the king personally to himself, but also, as the agrarian reforms of the eighteenth century showed, because absolutism in Denmark was consistent with regard for the welfare of the common people. But he was now a champion of freedom in church and state alike, and welcomed the new constitution of 1849 which admitted the people to a share in power.

The full significance of his action can only be appreciated if we bear in mind that by this time he was no mere private individual but commanded a large and influential following. In 1839 he had accepted an appointment as chaplain to a Copenhagen institution and in the church thus put at his disposal was able to gather round him a congregation largely composed of his disciples. Nor had he any longer to fear the opposition of the church authorities when he introduced his own hymns into the services. The order subjecting his writings to a censorship had been cancelled and he was in every way free, while enjoying royal support. In the Danish Church there was a Grundtvigian party, some of whose members rose to high office and whose work was profoundly influencing the religious life of the rural population. His participation in the political struggles of the time, though only a temporary one, was therefore of the greatest importance, for it showed that one could be at the same time a faithful son of the Church and an ardent advocate of the people's rights. Whereas in Germany

Lutheranism tended to ally itself with the forces of reaction under the slogan 'Throne and Altar', in the Scandinavian countries it was able to recognize in the movements for individual liberty, democracy, and social justice a spirit akin to its own.

It is instructive to read in Kierkegaard's *Journals* some of the reactions of another Dane to the events of the time. He has nothing but contempt for his people and the national enthusiasm which accompanied the war with the German states, while his sympathies are all with absolutism, a government that dares to govern and does not truckle to the masses. One can only be thankful that it was Grundtvig's interpretation of events which prevailed finally and not Kierkegaard's.

§

The appearance of Bismarck on the scene in 1862 made a peaceful solution of the vexed questions of the two duchies impossible. For he needed war, to strengthen the Prussian monarchy and army and to distract attention from his contempt for the constitution. On November 15th, 1863, Frederick VII died without male issue, and was succeeded by Christian IX in accordance with the terms of the Treaty of London. Bismarck seized the occasion to pick a quarrel and, in alliance with Austria, the Prussian army invaded Holstein. The Danes resisted in anticipation of help from England, but none was forthcoming, and after Jutland had been occupied they were compelled to ask for terms. The Danish king was forced to surrender Schleswig-Holstein to the victorious powers and the population over which he ruled was reduced by a stroke of the pen to three-fifths of what it had been at his accession.

It was an hour of utter humiliation for Denmark, thus not only stripped of territory but plainly reduced to insignificance. In Prussia an adversary had arisen with whom she could not hope to contend, while with the union of Germany a few years later she saw herself relegated to a place among those nations which live only by the sufferance of their neighbours. Only one form of resistance was possible to her, that of the spirit. As the best means of maintaining that spirit the Folk High School came into its own. Already in 1850 Kristen Kold, a man with a most romantic life-story, had opened a school for young peasants, both men and women, on the island of Funen, and one much nearer to Grundtvig's ideals than that at Rodding. Stirred at once by the preaching of a revivalist and the sagas of his people's heroic past, he was profoundly influenced by reading Grundtvig's *History of the World*, and dedicated his life to teaching on his discharge from service in the first war against the German states. Encouraged by the master, he opened his school with fifteen pupils and with no better accommodation than a small cottage, with the schoolroom on the ground floor and the bedroom (for teachers and pupils alike) in the loft.

Between 1844 and 1864 altogether eleven folk high-schools were opened in Denmark, while between 1865 and 1870 thirty more followed them. In nearly every case the men who founded these schools were young ministers or teachers who were ardent followers of Grundtvig; as he grew old his spirit entered into them and they were able to do the work of which he had only dreamed.

§

The last thirty years of Grundtvig's life were free from the storms which had beat upon him in his earlier years. He had become one of the most honoured names in the northern countries and some of the leading personalities of Denmark were among his followers, while the Norwegian poet Bjornsön saw in him his spiritual leader. Thanks to these men whom he had inspired, and who from time to time gathered round him in veneration, he influenced almost every aspect of life in his native country. On his seventieth birthday his admirers in Denmark and Norway presented him with a monetary gift to be used for the erection of a folk high-school; on the same occasion the king conferred upon him the honorary title of bishop. His first wife had died in 1851 and he married thereafter a second and a third time.

Old animosities too were dying down. More than once, during the campaign for national renewal, two men appeared side by side on the same platform. The one was Grundtvig, the other was that same Professor Clausen, on whom he had declared war in his rasher days. A change had now come over them both, and if the former had learned tolerance the latter had come, partly under the influence of his former critic, to see a new value in the tradition of the Church and the gospel of Martin Luther. Even a speculative theologian like Martensen, whose books have been translated into German and English, and who represented in his day the Hegelianizing tendency in theology, gladly acknowledged that, with all his faults, Grundtvig had upon him unmistakably the mark of a man raised up by God for the succour of his people. In striking and singularly appropriate language, he likened his great contemporary to an organ on which now a spirit from another world plays and now again some capricious musician from this world; he acted often without well knowing why he did so, as one who was used for purposes beyond his own by a higher power.

The Church of Denmark was taking on a new shape during Grundtvig's old age and very largely as a result of his influence: it achieved that remarkable synthesis of the two conflicting principles of state establishment and congregational independency of which more will be said in the sequel. His hymns too had found a place in the worship of his fellow-countrymen and passed on into the servicebooks of the other Scandinavian churches.

The mood which governed the last thirty years of his life is nowhere more clearly revealed to us than in a series of lectures given in Copenhagen in 1838, embodying the reminiscences of half a century. He looks back upon the past with a generous wisdom and surveys the future with an optimism which does much to explain that youthfulness of spirit which enabled him to gather the most ardent youth of the day around him even when he had long passed the normal human span of life. Looking back on the French Revolution with the eyes of a seer, he interprets it as the judgement of God upon unjust rule and a warning against a similar misuse of power in other lands. To Napoleon he assigns a place among the great figures of world history and demands that if the historian is allowed to throw a veil over the failings of a Caesar, he should not be expected to expose those of a breaker and maker of nations in his own day. He speaks of the illumination which came to him and enabled him to discern in the present and in the life of the common people precisely those elements of greatness which others can only find in the past. It is ingratitude to the generations which bore us and disservice to those which will come after us, to turn away thus from the present, for it is the one field of action assigned to us by Providence and of it we have no right to despair. Yes, he himself, after long wandering in the past and in the history of other lands, has come home to Denmark and the present, and has come home full of hope. It is no foolish optimism which he cherishes, for those who are familiar with his career will remember how he never scrupled to scourge the sins of his time and how his harp was tuned to strife between gods and giants, life and death. In him now life has conquered death, memory and hope combine in the acknowledgement of the present hour and the present opportunity as all that a man should desire who is willing to do the work to which he is called. Not in past ages, not with heroes of old, do we live; let our hearts be filled with hope, for the Golden Age is about to dawn, the age whose sons will be as valiant and as noble as their sires ever were.

§

With this unconquerable spirit he moved on towards the end of life, a patriarch surrounded by the veneration of his followers. We have a picture of him as he was in the last week or so of his life; it is drawn by Edmund Gosse and is worth quoting in full. He describes how he waited in the little chapel so long that it seemed as though the preacher would be unable to come.

> 'Suddenly, and when we had given up all hope, there entered from the vestry and walked rapidly to the altar a personage who seemed to me the oldest man I had ever seen. He prayed in a few words that sounded as if they came from underground, and then he turned and exhorted the communicants in the same slow, dull voice. He stood beside me for a moment as he laid his hands on a girl's head, and I saw his face to perfection. For a man of ninety he could not be called infirm, but the attention was drawn less to his vitality, great as it was, than to his appearance of excessive age. He looked like a troll from some cave in Norway; he might have been centuries old. From the vast orb of his bald head, very long silky hair, perfectly white, fell over his shoulders, and mingled with a long and loose white beard. His eyes flamed under very beetling brows, and they were the only part of his face that seemed alive, even when he spoke. His features were still shapely, but colourless and dry, like parchment. I never saw so strange a head. When he rose into the pulpit, and began to preach, and in his dead voice warned us all to

beware of false spirits, he looked very noble, but the nobility was scarcely Christian. In the body of the church he had reminded me of a troll; in the pulpit he looked more like some forgotten druid, that had survived from Mona and could not die.'

On September 2nd, 1872, the end came. His chaplain and his son had taken their turns reading to him, when at three o'clock in the afternoon he announced that he was tired and would rest. A few minutes later he had passed away peacefully, sitting in his arm-chair. The warrior had gone to his rest.

4

Odin and Christ

GRUNDTVIG'S passion for the myths and legends of the North began at his mother's knee in the Udby manse; when he went on to the grammar school it seemed incredible that anyone should ask him to exchange the virile warriors of Denmark's past for the stiff and posturing figures of ancient Rome. At the university, while he was nominally preparing for the ministry, this remained the only study which attracted him, and during his stay as tutor on Langeland he was able to return in imagination and research to this land of his first enthusiasms. He became in those days no mere admirer of the gods and heroes, but their ardent devotee; the old religion actually came to life in his soul and battle was joined once more between Odin and Christ. In after days he came to look back with regret upon the 'heathenism' of this period, but the old gods were never really expelled from his life, they were subdued to a *praeparatio evangelica* rather. In the spiritual development of this man Odin began as a peer of Christ, but ended by laying down his sword before the Cross.

Grundtvig's *Mythology of the North* is considered by many as his masterpiece. It appeared first in 1808 but was reissued in greatly enlarged form in 1832. The author reveals himself as a unique combination of the poet and the historian. On the one hand, he undertakes an enquiry into the sources, age, and authenticity of the various sagas; on the other hand, he attempts a bold imaginative reconstruction of the ancient myths as parts of a single grandiose whole. As regards his critical work, later scholarship has found much in his work to reject but not a little also to accept. He erred often as the result of the presuppositions, partly Christian in origin and partly derived from the romantic temper, with which he approached his work. He read back a primitive monotheism into the sagas and while he was aware of Christian interpolations in them, he overlooked the possibility that the new faith might have influenced the old one in subtle ways before finally dispossessing it. Sometimes too the poet got the better of the scholar and he would argue that because some lines were peculiarly vigorous they must be original, and would brush aside as mere pedantry the appeal to manuscript readings.

In the second edition of the book he adopts an approach to the myths which clearly owes a great deal to Herder and his conception of history as the divine education of the human race in its various groupings. For Herder, the spirit of a people finds expression in its customs, rites, and myths; all is indeed the unfolding, stage by stage, of what was from the beginning implicit therein. The character of a people is thus revealed to us in the tales which its mothers tell to their children, the songs which accompany its festive occasions, and the folk-ways which continue unchanged from generation to generation. As the myths of a people are, so is that people.

For Grundtvig therefore the ancient sagas of his native land were as a mirror in which the essential qualities of the Danish people could be observed. They belonged to their unspoilt childhood, before they were contaminated by alien and injurious influences, to those spacious days when life was lived in a freedom, a heroism, and a faith which put to shame the weakness of our degenerate days. The myths of each people, he declared, are the peculiar sanctuary of its spirit and its truest self-revelation: as such they are also prophetic, foreshadowing what may come of it. They are full of the promise of youth, the ideals and hopes which may indeed go unfulfilled but which nevertheless belong to the people in its essential self as the distortions and half-achievements of a later period do not.

It is therefore the view of life which is native to the northern peoples, their inborn heroism, which comes to expression in their tales of gods and heroes. They have seen more clearly than any other people that the lot of man in this world is one of struggle, that here our strength is to be tried to the utmost and that wisdom lies in the glad acceptance of such trial. Beyond us and in another world peace may lie, but in this world we are summoned to accept life as a thing of risk and challenge and to count it all honour that such exacting tasks are assigned to us.

> *Sound, sound the clarion, fill the fife;*
> *To all the sensual world proclaim:*
> *One crowded hour of glorious life*
> *Is worth an age without a name.*

In the edition of 1832 an attempt is made to carry through a symbolic interpretation of the myths, with results which must seem at times fantastic. Some spiritual equivalent is assigned to each of the gods: Odin becomes inspiration, Thor's hammer truth, and Valhalla an assurance of immortality. We feel on more solid ground when he allegorizes the life of the gods in Valhalla, with its combat renewed each day and its feasts on the never-to-be-consumed boar's flesh. This brings to expression that conflict of good against evil from which there is no release for man in this world, a conflict that only appears to die down with advancing age, since a new generation must wage it afresh for itself. That the dead rise again from the battlefield to take their places again next day in the combat is the apt symbol of this fact that humanity as it renews itself from generation to generation is committed continually afresh to the heroic struggle for the divine in itself against the forces of evil which surge against it. As Lehmann has said, for us the symbolism is of secondary value, what interests us is the faith which is expressed by means of it and can exist without it, the valiant acceptance of life as a theatre of spiritual warfare and the unquenchable hope of victory by which such courage is sustained. In this magnificent conception all the various elements are expressed which entered into the personality of Grundtvig: the moral idealism of Fichte joins hands with the romanticism of Schelling and the ancient heathenism of the North enlists in the service of Christ. Valhalla has become an ante-chamber of the Kingdom of Heaven!

What facilitated more than anything else this reconciliation of old and new, this acceptance by Odin of his master Christ, was the part assigned in the sagas to Ragnarok, the twilight of the gods. At the last, so it was prophesied, Loki would be released from his bonds and would lead the giants to battle against the gods. In that day of slaughter, the warriors on both sides would perish by mutual destruction. Only some few of the gods would escape and with them a new age would dawn after the ruin of the old world. In the language of the Prose Edda: 'In that time the earth shall emerge out of the sea, and shall then be green and fair; then shall the fruits of it be brought forth unsown.' The sons of Thor will come thither, Balder and his wife will join them from the land of the dead: a new and fairer sun will shine and the human race will people the earth again. What more fitting symbol could be found for the passing of one faith and the coming of another and more enduring one?

As Grundtvig read the sagas, they contained a whole tragic story of guilt and doom, but a doom redeemed by hope. The ancient gods perished by the sin of pride, daring to set themselves in opposition to the All-Father. Therefore the Norns direct the course of events so that gods and giants perish together in the final battle for supremacy. Or, in other words, the religion of the Norse peoples was superseded by Christianity, not owing to some turn of fortune or political exigency, but because it was no longer able to satisfy the spiritual needs of those who gave it allegiance. They needed something purer and nobler, but this could only come by the breakdown of everything in which they had hitherto believed.

But the Christ who vanquished Odin was his fulfilment as well as his mortal foe: the heroic virtues remained, to be employed in a better service. And Christ himself for Grundtvig took over some of the features of the one whom he had dethroned. In his poems and hymns he celebrates Christ as the hero, the mighty warrior who in the grim struggle with death has vanquished it once for all and emerged triumphant in the resurrection. 'He fought as a hero, lived and died as a hero should. His life was a deed, a knightly deed, by which he won the victory for himself and for us all.' Crowned with thorns and sentenced to death, he yet wins our homage as the world's true king. In one of his Easter poems, he tells how the centurion by the Cross saluted in the dying man the demigod, 'bold as a hero and as full of love as any woman.' But perhaps the noblest expression of this conception of Christ is in his translation and adaptation of the old English poem on the Harrowing of Hell. The devils howl as Christ knocks at the gate and it flies open to admit the conqueror. In the depths of hell he meets with the mother of all mankind, and Eve bows in wonder and adoration before the son who is at the same time her deliverer. One kiss, and she is free from her bondage; the exalted Lord returns in victory with the train of the glorified accompanying him. The Christ who redeemed mankind has taken up into himself something of the Thor whose hammer slew the giants.

In Björnson's epic *Arnljot Gelline* the Christianity of Grundtvig takes flesh before us in the persons of Olaf the Holy and the men who follow him. The poem belongs to the period in which the Norwegian poet was among the most devoted followers of the great Dane. 'The Grundtvigian view of Christianity and history stamps the entire work. For Grundtvig, God is the people's leader throughout the course of history, with whom men ally themselves of their own free will, as the warriors of old took service with a king, as free men giving him their full devotion. In this spirit of free devotion, men bring with them their full human equipment, but all human effort becomes ennobled by the divine relation.' So, in the dream of Arnljot, he sees how all the impulses of his nature which had hitherto run riot in revenge and pillage can be disciplined to nobler purposes as they are employed in the service of Christ's man, King Olaf.

> *Was it only a dream that passed before me,*
> *Yet was it more than all my waking;*
> *It was life itself. . . .*
> *The life I will henceforth live!*
> *Olaf Haraldsson, King of Norway,*
> *He it was;—him have I chosen!*
> *He has strength that is not his own,*
> *A higher goal than aught I have aimed at.*
> *Him must I cleave to.*

With this reference to Björnson we are led on to a consideration, first, of Grundtvig's conception of history, and then of his view of the Christian as the crown and fulfilment of the truly human. His *Handbook of World-History* was published in three stout volumes between 1833 and 1835 and displays the same combination of mastery of the sources and comprehensive vision as his *Mythology of the North*. But it was characteristic of him that he found his sources rather among the songs and legends of the people or in early chronicles than in official archives. He wrote history as a poet, and what concerned him was the development of peoples rather than the achievements of individuals. Here again of course the influence of Herder is to be traced in the principles with which he went to work. In his *Ideas on the Philosophy of History* (1784–91) Herder saw in the drama of world-history a unity and a development of humanity according to fixed laws. 'In history as in nature all develops out of certain natural conditions according to fixed laws. The law of progress in history rests on a similar law in nature, which is active from the outset, though obscurely, in the powers of inorganic nature and their products, which the scientist is familiar with in the ascending series of organic beings, and which the historian perceives in the spiritual strivings of the human race. History is progressive development to humanity.'

But Herder's ideas had passed through the mind of Fichte before they reached Grundtvig. Fichte took over from Kant the conception of an ideal state, a state based on moral principle and reconciling freedom and authority, as the goal of world history: he also attempted a psychological account of the development of humanity from instinct to self-conscious reason. In accordance with his basic position of the absolute freedom of the self, he attached less importance than Herder did to the natural setting in which a people must live its life. 'It is not the sea that produces the Vikings, but the Vikings find in the sea the element which corresponds to their nature, their symbol.'

In the same way as his predecessors, Grundtvig saw in world-history a universal drama in which the actors are not individuals but peoples. Three peoples in particular are the bearers of history, the Jews, the Greeks, and the northern group of nations. Each people hands on its achievements to those who come after it, and the nations of modern Europe are thus enriched by the effort and experience of all who went before them. But the attention of the historian is confined to those who stand in this way in the main stream of western civilization: others, not only the Indians and the Chinese, but even the Arabs and the Turks, are passed over as never having entered into the great column as it marches down the ages. History begins with the Bible, and it is made by those who accept the Bible and build its teaching into their life. The picture which Grundtvig thus reaches is attained, it will be seen, by a process of selection which will appear arbitrary to those who do not share the point of view with which he approaches his material.

That point of view is twofold. In the first place, it is psychological. Humanity as a whole goes through the same three phases as those which characterize the development of the individual; it has its youth, manhood, and old age. To each of these a specific psychological trait is assigned: youth is the period of imagination, manhood of feeling, and old age of reflection and thought. In accordance with this scheme, classical antiquity is treated as the youth of the race and the rich mythology of the ancient world is cited as evidence for the correctness of this classification. The medieval period is then described as pre-eminently that of feeling: to be sure, Grundtvig has to strain the theory somewhat at this point, since, as a good Protestant, he must reserve the full manhood of the European peoples for the Reformation. In characterizing the modern period as that of reflection, he shows himself at once a child and a critic of the eighteenth century.

What is true of the human race as a whole is equally true of its component peoples. Here also Grundtvig deals with the facts in somewhat magisterial fashion to make them fit the framework he has designed in advance for them. Thus, he finds in the history of each nation the corresponding periods of youth, maturity, and age, accompanied by fantasy, feeling, and reflection respectively. Lehmann remarks that we must understand 'feeling' in a wider sense than is usual with ourselves, and that we must think of humanity in each of its phases as willing and active, though the will is determined in one phase by one psychical trait and in another by another. Man of action as he himself was,

Grundtvig cannot have meant to exclude the will from his psychological analysis, he must have presupposed it.

In the second place, Grundtvig approaches history from a specifically theological angle. Man in each generation is set between the possibilities of faith and unbelief. The will of God is not imposed upon events by an external Providence but is their inner meaning; there is in history something of what Arnold Toynbee has taught us to speak of as 'challenge and response'. There are peoples who have met the challenge of God in events and others who have failed to do so. Thus the Jews are the people of faith *par excellence*, as the Romans are above all others the people of unbelief. The French are cold sceptics, the Germans warm-hearted and men of faith. It is the same with the various periods of history. The middle ages, of course, was the age of faith, while the modern world had fallen away to unbelief. The result is a number of sweeping judgements on collectivities and centuries which it would be difficult to substantiate: Grundtvig was not of Burke's opinion and he was always ready to draw up an indictment against a whole nation.

It was particularly the Romans who roused his ire, and after them the French. In his hostility to Rome he followed Herder, who saw in the imperial city by the Tiber not the civilizing force which had held the world together for centuries, but the mailed heel which trampled upon the freedom and life of Carthage, the Greek city-states, Jerusalem, and many other centres of culture which Rome could do nothing to replace. France was scorned as the land of prose and reason, with wit but without genius, capable of mediocre achievement but with no sense for the highest things.

To these two peoples Grundtvig opposed two others, the Greeks and the race from which he himself sprang. Like Fichte, he beheld in the barbarians not the destroyers but the renewers of civilization: familiar as he was from boyhood with the sagas of the North, he was able to do justice to the importance of these peoples and his account of them forms one of the most valuable sections of his work. Among them, of course, the Danes are 'the chosen people'! His love for Greece—a trait which again he shared with Herder—led him to make the extraordinary suggestion that modern Greek should take the place of Latin as the common language of the educated class!

History as Grundtvig understood it was no mere succession of events to be mastered by the secular intelligence and judged by cold reason: the presence of God was in it from beginning to end. Yet what he offered his time was no merely ecclesiastical version of the past: the world does not for him exist for the sake of the Church. Rather is the protagonist in the drama of universal history civil society as such. 'Enlightened by the school and freed by the Church, civil society moves on the frontier between the visible and the invisible worlds, the world of the hand and the world of the spirit. It is this which constitutes it the proper subject of universal history. But it is equally true that the genuine state is only to be found where all these three are, with the true Church and the true school constantly accompanying it and conferring their benefits upon it.'

There is no closer parallel to Grundtvig among modern historians than the man who resembles him in certain other respects, our own Thomas Carlyle. In each we meet with the same prophetic interpretation of the past, the same conviction that 'this world's history is its judgement too', and the same combination of scientific research and didactic purpose. But, as Lehmann points out, one great difference between the two is in their evaluation of Rome, which Grundtvig abhors, but of which Carlyle speaks with enthusiastic admiration. It is significant in this connection that Grundtvig blames the British for not having remained faithful to their nordic heritage: instead they have assimilated the Latin tradition, which is responsible also for French scepticism and the superficialities of the Age of Reason.

§

The final question here is that of the relation between the human and the Christian. Grundtvig's whole life can be viewed as an effort to find an answer to this question. The same could be said of his enigmatic contemporary Kierkegaard. The difference between the two men is worth nothing here especially. The latter came to Christianity through a study of classical antiquity and German philosophy: he set Christ over against Socrates, the Incarnation in contrast with the religion of immanence. He seems to have had little or no understanding for the world of myth and legend in which the other found one of the sources of his spiritual life. Nor was Kierkegaard ever able to come to a satisfactory solution of his problem. While at one time he regarded the highest human possibility as a stage which needed to be gone through before the true Christian standpoint could be reached (though the one must not be regarded as a development of the other but rather as a leap beyond it as religion of any kind is a leap ahead of the ethical life), in the end he saw the two in stark antagonism. In his final assault upon the Church, he championed a Christ whose commands would mean the extinction of the human race; he brands woman as a snare of the devil and marriage as a sin.

In spite of the pathological element in his make-up, Grundtvig's outlook on life was fundamentally a healthy one, and he was accordingly spared the soul-struggles through which Kierkegaard went, as he was saved from so disastrous a conclusion as that at which he arrived. We might summarize his position by saying that he combined Fichte and Rousseau, the moral earnestness of the one and the love of freedom of the other, reverence before all that is great and holy and trust in one's native impulses. Like the Apostle Paul, he was able to decry outward constraint because he was capable of being a law to himself: the good was no mere obligation but a joy. And Christ came, not to destroy, but to fulfil, whatever is of worth in human life.

One of the favourite words of Grundtvig was 'life', and in that he summed up just that combination of moral earnestness and freedom which was characteristic of him. He saw the world as a battle-ground on which life was continually at grips with death, and man as called to take part in this struggle for the overcoming of death by life. In 1836 the Lutheran Church in Denmark celebrated the tercentenary of the Reformation. A deputation from Berlin came to Copenhagen for the occasion, and one of its members was Professor Marheinecke, the leading exponent of that speculative theology which sought to enlist the Hegelian philosophy in the service of Christianity. The visitor from Germany went to see Grundtvig and spoke to him of the achievements of the speculative theology and how it could resolve even such an antithesis as that of thought and being in a higher and inclusive unity. The Dane replied that such flights were not for him, his concern was elsewhere: 'my opposition is life and death!' To the end of his days he was just such a fighter for truth against the lie, for life against death, as he saw symbolized in those heroes of Valhalla who, cut down in the combat of to-day, would rise again to-morrow to renew the struggle.

But life meant for him also freedom and creativity, the flash of insight by which truth is discerned and the glad action which gives expression to it. Truth was a thing to be grasped by the whole personality, the response of one's manhood to God's self-disclosure, never a proposition to be got by heart. Only life can communicate life—that was the basic thought alike in his work for the renewal of church life among the people and in his advocacy of a new and liberating system of education. Hence his impassioned advocacy of freedom in the final phase of his career: he would give freedom to error even, since he was confident that it would be overcome in the end by truth. Hence his hatred of compulsion in religious matters as the very path to hell.

He carried this love of freedom into the sphere of morality, where he was opposed to anything resembling the ascetic and monastic discipline of Catholicism. The body was God's creation and should be used in his service, not abused as enticement to sin. The whole idea of the government of life by rule and precept was alien to him, and in one of his poems he satirically compares the rationalistic exhortations to virtue with which he was familiar in his student days (and which, to be sure, he had at one time employed!) to the slavery of the Hebrews in Egypt. Conscience was the seat of moral authority: the true man has an inner law which he is glad to obey and needs not to have one imposed upon him from without. He had learned from the New Testament that one simple precept suffices for the whole duty of man, the precept of love for one's neighbour. 'Love is the fulfilment of the law and the promise of perfection; it alone is God's will and the fruit of his Spirit.' Christian morality is not obedience to law but the free living-out of an impulse towards the good; it does not copy the virtues of others but is spontaneous and creative in all that it does. Across the centuries Grundtvig joins hands with Paul, the apostle of freedom.

In all this we can doubtless trace the influence ultimately of Rousseau, but what Grundtvig derived from him had been thoroughly christianized in the process. He did not share, as Kierkegaard did, the pessimistic Lutheran estimate of human nature: he spoke of the dogma that the image of God in man had been obliterated by the Fall as the great error of Lutheranism. In the controversy between Erasmus and Luther he would no doubt have been found on the side of the former; in his teaching he is more concerned with the possibilities of human nature than its shortcomings. He is convinced of the essential nobility of man. He is emphatic that, with all his weakness, man can respond to God and so rise to higher levels. 'God's voice rang over the dust when he created Adam, and even to this day some echo of it hovers over us; even to this day it lives on our tongue and men sing of it with joy: for we are God's image.' Man is so great because he is a vehicle of the Spirit and, as we shall see, it was as Spirit that Grundtvig thought of God.

It is because he has this strong sense that man is God's creature, that he is made in God's image and that God's Spirit is continually at work within him, that Grundtvig can put such trust in the common people and in human nature. He is sure that what is in man is good and from God, therefore he can demand that it should be given freedom to develop itself. Free himself from tortuous scruples, he was able to accept himself from God's hands, with his powers and his limitations, and was willing to be simply what God had made him to be. He knows, to be sure, the reality of sin and death, but for him these are enemies who must and can be overcome, they are not tyrannies which hold the race in their grip. There was in him, too, something of the moral courage which rejoiced in the very difficulties of life, as a Viking wished for yet more enemies that he might prove his manhood by overcoming them all.

In all this, however, he was no individualist in the sense of pitting the individual against society. He himself found self-fulfilment by accepting his place among his people and devoting his life to their service, while Kierkegaard regretted all his days that he had not been born in a country more appreciative of his genius and providing a larger public for his message. 'He wanted to do justice to the individual in all his specific qualities, yet without being properly speaking an individualist. He always sees man within the race and as a member of the race, as a citizen and a member of the community. But just because he has confidence in this totality in which he stands, he loosens the fetters which are upon man and sets him free to live, to think, to feel, to act as he will. There is no room here for any constraint, no discipline strictly speaking, scarcely even proper instruction. He risks everything on the conviction that, if only a chance to grow is given, the growth will at once be in the right direction. That is why he can grant freedom to Loki and freedom to Thor; for he is quite convinced that Thor will very soon finish with Loki.'

It is a bold vision of human possibilities, but it is a Christian vision and not merely borrowed from Rousseau. And that it was by no means without justification a study of Grundtvig's influence upon his own country will amply show.

5

Church and People

'FIRST a man and then a Christian.' In this maxim of his, Grundtvig has given expression to one of his ruling ideas. The Christian is something distinct from the human, God's grace rather than man's achievement, nevertheless the latter is a necessary preliminary stage to the former. Only he who has mastered life's elementary but all-important lessons of sincerity and courage, the service of truth and fellowship with his kind, can enter with profit into the school of the Gospel. But his understanding of humanity was sharply opposed to that of rationalism; the individual exists, not in abstraction from, but rather embedded in, the historical community of the nation. The human lies, for the Dane, in the cultivation of what is distinctively Danish, and to ape an alien culture is to commit the sin of selling one's birthright. God's will is for variety, for the full development of the characteristics intrinsic to each people, not for their obliteration in the name of a cosmopolitanism which has no blood in its veins and is incapable of any grand passion. While therefore he sometimes used exaggerated language of the Danish people, that is to be set down to his temperament, always inclined to hyperbole and poetic language; the kind of nationalism which he preached was quite consistent with a genuine world loyalty.

He wanted therefore a Danish Christianity for the Danish people, one in which the natural gifts which he had seen and loved among them would be put at the service of the Gospel. But he would have had no sympathy with that incredible amalgam of heathenism and Lutheranism of which the 'German Christians' were guilty when Hitler's star was in the ascendant. As we shall see in the next chapter, what he specially valued in Christianity is just what is common to Christians in all generations and all nationalities, what even transcends the division of Christendom between Catholic and Protestant, Lutheran and Reformed. As a young poet, he might speak of Odin and Christ as two sons of the common Father, but as a preacher and church leader he had a strong sense of the authority of Christianity as something which God gives and man receives; nowhere does he introduce the ancient religion into that world which was sacred for him, the world of the Bible and the Church's hymn-book, the Apostles' Creed and Luther's faith. What he wanted was what the wisest leaders of the Church in the Far East want to-day, the expression of a universal Christianity in forms which spring out of the life of the people and which will therefore enable it to enter into and redeem that life.

For this consecration of the Danish genius to Christ an instrument was already available in the state church. As in other European countries, the opposing fronts at the Reformation were of social and political, as well as religious, alignment. The new faith served as a weapon in the king's struggle against the aristocracy and the higher clergy, and he was able to rely for support on the middle-class and the peasants. One king was driven from the country for his attempts to reform the church, but the controversy was decided in the royal favour when in 1536 Christian III resorted to the drastic measure of ordering the arrest of the bishops. The new church constitution, which was introduced in the following year on the advice of Bugenhagen and given legal force in 1539, broke entirely with the episcopal succession. 'It did not set up a new church with an independent organization but established a national religion, with the national government pledged to uphold it.' The process thus began was carried farther when in 1660 the monarchy was made absolute. By the law of 1683

Lutheranism became the sole type of religion tolerated within the country, except for the privileges granted to foreign ambassadors. The royal authority within the church was supreme and unlimited: it had the sole right to legislate for its affairs, to appoint and depose its officials, the bishops included. The clergy were bound by the Augsburg Confession and restricted to the use of authorized liturgical forms. In practice, a certain modification of this system accompanied the rationalism of the eighteenth century, but religious liberty was only conceded at law in 1849, and Grundtvig has an honourable place among those who worked to secure this.

To be sure, in the earlier part of his career he was disposed, as we have seen, to use this authoritarian system against his theological opponents. In the Clausen case, he had argued that a minister of the state church who had departed from that allegiance to Scripture and Lutheran orthodoxy to which his ordination vows committed him should be deposed by the government. On that occasion he had anticipated his subsequent development by declaring war on all rationalizing tendencies within the church in the name of the Apostles' Creed. His attack on Clausen had failed, however, while his opponent continued to train the ministry of the church. As the result of this experience, and also of what he had learned from his journeys to England, he changed his policy completely and became a champion of liberty and a comprehensive church.

From this point on, he demanded full liberty for groups and individuals within the established church: it must provide a home for orthodox and rationalists alike. To grant freedom to both parties was to take the surest step towards the final victory of truth; at the same time, perhaps the one party needed freedom as much as the other, if not more so. He did not question the state church: it was necessary in order, by its parochial system, to reach the people in town and countryside. But it must not use its influence in favour of any one section, but must allow liberty of expression alike to those who stand in the old ways and to those who question them. That included the relaxation of the rule that the people of a parish must worship only under the parish minister. Why, he urged, should not a group of orthodox folk in one neighbourhood, if they are unable to profit spiritually by the ministrations of a rationalist pastor, be able to call in a pastor from another who will confirm them in their faith? And why should the clergy themselves be bound by formulae which they can only accept with mental reservations? Why confine them to the use of liturgical forms which may or may not correspond to their personal convictions? He wanted thus to preserve the structure of the establishment while filling it with a new life in freedom; he wanted, in other words, to change an authoritarian church into a comprehensive one.

Danish religious life had always been open to influences from beyond the borders, especially from Germany and our own country. These in some cases brought into existence groups of people who met to encourage each other in the Christian life but who remained as before loyal adherents of the state church. Baptist propaganda introduced a new feature, as those who were won by this refused to bring their children to be baptized and so challenged the existing system, under which all children of Christian parents were required to be baptized according to the Lutheran rite. The presiding bishop at the time was Mynster, an eloquent preacher who exercised a great influence upon Kierkegaard at one time, but whom he denounced unmercifully after his death. Mynster was intensely conservative in matters of church government and wished to have the law enforced: one of Grundtvig's followers, the brother of Sören Kierkegaard, refused to baptize a child against the wishes of the parent and was threatened with deposition by Mynster.

But before the incident was settled the changes of 1848 created an entirely new situation and the law of 1849 granted religious liberty to non-Lutherans.

This law recognized the Lutheran as the national church of Denmark and proposed to provide it with a constitution. But the laws necessary for this were not passed and the discussion on the relation of church to state showed such diversity of opinion in the Diet that matters were left much where they were. Indeed, it has been maintained that the church lost rather than gained by the transition from royal control to a supervision shared by the king with the Diet, for the members of the latter are not necessarily members of the Lutheran Church, as the king is required by law to be. Church matters are in the hands of a cabinet minister, and it is on his advice that clergy are appointed by the king. Government and Diet legislate for the church, which has no organ of self-government: an advisory council of bishops and university professors was set up in 1883, but it was dissolved in 1901. Nevertheless, within this apparently rigid system there is abundant room for liberty of conscience and full play for congregational life.

To this result Kierkegaard as well as Grundtvig has no doubt contributed. In the closing phase of his life he launched a fierce and uncompromising attack on the whole principle of the establishment as inimical to any genuine Christianity. He refused to recognize the claim of Denmark or any country to the adjective 'Christian', since only the individual could have faith. He branded as shameful betrayals of the Christian name those great churches which gathered everyone into them at baptism and offered a livelihood and honours to those who would make a career of the preaching of the Cross. In the series of broadsheets which he was publishing at the time of his death he demanded the separation of church and state and the abolition of infant baptism. His attacks upon the clergy were particularly virulent, and when Martensen succeeded Mynster as bishop and described his predecessor in his funeral sermon as a faithful witness to Christ, Kierkegaard's indignation knew no bounds. His ideas worked as a ferment among the youth of his time, and if they won some among them for a more earnest-minded discipleship, there were others whom he repelled so that they forsook the Church altogether. The philosopher Höffding, for example, tells us that he began by accepting Kierkegaard's version of Christianity as the only possible one and so was drawn to it, but that he ended by rejecting it and turning instead to humanism.

The Danish State Church as it exists to-day is in many respects unique among establishments. The most recent legislation was passed in the first two decades of this century and brought into existence parochial councils which have charge of local business, though they have no powers of discipline over the incumbent. When a living falls vacant, the council has the right to submit three names from which the Ministry for Church Affairs will choose one; if the council unites on a single nominee, the ministry will accept him. The councils can also suggest names for a vacant episcopal see, and have certain rights of voting. But the most remarkable feature of the system, and the one which is plainly of Grundtvig's inspiration, is the legal guarantee of minority rights. If five heads of families so desire, they can invite a minister other than the one in their parish to preach, celebrate baptism or communion, or perform other functions, using for those purposes the parish church. If ten church members wish, they can form a voluntary congregation, with the right to call their own minister (who must have the same qualifications as those required for the state-supported clergy) and to use the parish church for their services. If twenty heads of families wish to invite a second minister acceptable to themselves, they can do so, and his stipend will be paid as to one half by those who call him and as to one half by the state. But the clergy are still bound by the Augsburg Confession, though in no very restrictive sense, and Grundtvig's demand for alternative liturgical forms has not been met.

The picture thus sketched is that of a comprehensive church, and to that extent it is one with which we are already familiar in this country. The Danish Church of to-day has three main parties, of which the Grundtvigian is one. At the other extreme stands the Inner Mission, a revivalist and philanthropic movement associated with the name of William Beck. Grundtvig himself was not in sympathy with this movement, yet others have detected in it not a little of his spirit as well as something also which derives from Kierkegaard. Between the two stands what may be called the Centre party, which continues the tradition of Mynster and Martensen and is loyal to the old principles of the state church. These three parties are held together in the unity of a single organization, precisely as is the case with our own Church of England.

Yet the degree of comprehensiveness which has been achieved in Denmark far surpasses what has been found possible among ourselves. Denmark has its free churches, but these touch only a tiny minority of the population: the census gives 97 per cent. as the proportion connected with the state church. But it hardly needs such bodies, for it has admitted the principle of independency into the territory of establishment, as the legislation described above clearly shows. Why break with the establishment when it is so generous in its treatment of minority groups? What is there to contend for which it has not already in substance conceded?

It is clear that what lies behind Grundtvig's proposals for reform is a frank acceptance of the dualism of the visible and the invisible Church. To some this will seem his crowning error, while others will see in it another proof of a strong sense for the realities of the situation with which he was dealing. The state church might remain—to use Hölderlin's expression for the state—as 'the hedge about the garden of life': it was the necessary organization of manpower and finance. But within it the spiritual life would be maintained by the voluntary activities of the congregation, which was the real unit of Christian fellowship. The great advantage of the state was that it could afford to be neutral as against conflicting opinions within the church, while self-government might prove only another name for party-strife. The inner life of the church would be the care of the congregation.

Grundtvig's position was perhaps illogical: ought he not to have demanded a greater degree of accordance between inner and outer? I suspect, however, that in these matters logical consistency is not the best of criteria. It would seem as though, for anything like its adequate expression, Christianity needs both the Church and the sect, the mass-institution which introduces each generation afresh to the Gospel and the smaller group of convinced and committed individuals. Of these neither can lay claim to a monopoly of the truth, but each should recognize that the other is also of God and does his work. In England the Established Church and the Free Churches exist side by side, both of them mixed types but the one more church than sect and the other to-day passing from the stage of the sect to that of the church. The two principles of state support and voluntaryism are for us expressed in two different types of association. The Danish experiment has shown that this is not necessary, that one and the same institution can contain both, that it is possible to be a Congregationalist within an established church. It is one of the outstanding merits of Grundtvig that he did so much to make this possible, providing us thus with a pattern of unity in which diversity is not merely tolerated but actually encouraged.

6

The Living Word

THE last chapter will have been wholly misleading if it has left on the reader's mind the impression that Grundtvig's work for the Church was done in the sphere of organization. That was but the least part of his achievement, and we have now to describe how he sent through the religious life of his country a new impulse of spiritual vitality and fervour. The party which derives its name from him remains to this day as the champion of an original and highly important conception of Christianity, orthodox in the sense that its roots are in the past, but progressive also, inasmuch as its allegiance is given rather to the continuous life of the Christian Church in all lands and all ages than to any particular doctrinal formulation.

We have seen how his conversion brought Grundtvig to a literalism in his treatment of the Bible and a harshness in his opposition to those who employed critical methods of Bible-study. It was in this mood that he challenged Clausen, branding him as a traitor to the Gospel and declaring that to tolerate him within the Church would be to degrade it to the level of an idol-temple. He took his stand then on the Bible, but he used language at the time which makes it clear that he was already seeking his authority elsewhere. In a letter to Steffens, for example, he faces the fact that any appeal to the Bible is attended with the difficulty that someone has to decide what books fall within the Bible, and that, unless one follows Catholicism at this point and accepts the authority of the Church, one has to rely upon some sort of scholarly judgement. He is prepared for that and expresses his confidence that faith is not imperilled by such a conclusion, though he does not say how he conceives the reconciliation of the two to be effected. Again, as against Clausen, he declared that if he was not willing to be bound by the *regula fidei*, he (Grundtvig) could not accept him as a fellow-Christian. Here the emphasis shifts for the time being from the Bible to the Creed. It was in this second position that Grundtvig finally came to rest.

The polemic against Clausen and the rationalizing tendency in theology led him, therefore, to a decision on a question which was already agitating him: can the authority of Scripture be maintained as final and as the basis of the Church? He came to the conclusion that it could not. As long as appeal was made to Scripture, rationalism had unanswerable arguments at its disposal. It had only to say that the Danish version did not faithfully reproduce the original, that a knowledge of Hebrew would dispose of this messianic prophecy and a study of the New Testament in Greek would deprive that doctrine of the Trinity of this proof-text—and what could the ordinary person say in reply? He was equally helpless when the argument turned on the authenticity of a particular book or the order in which the various parts of the Bible were written. The net result therefore of repudiating the Papacy to make room for the Bible was that, through the Bible itself, one was left at the mercy of a new papacy—the consensus of opinion among scholars. And when that consensus was not forthcoming, one was lost! The Reformation had proposed to establish in the Church the priesthood of believers by putting the Bible in the hands of each member, so that he might win from it first-hand assurance of his salvation. But it now appeared that the Bible as he knew it was not capable of giving him certainty and that he could only find it by submitting himself to the few trained theologians who were competent to say what the Bible really means.

Such a state of things was intolerable for Grundtvig: like a genuine Lutheran he sought for a ground of assurance.

He needed, and he was convinced that the Church needed, some authority which lay beyond questioning as the basis of the spiritual life. Where was that to be found? The answer came in what he always spoke of as his 'incomparable discovery' and this fell either in 1825 or in 1826. He appealed from the letter of Scripture to 'the living word', the Church's confession of faith as it had gone down the centuries, renewed continually at the baptismal font. The final court of appeal is the Apostles' Creed as used in the baptismal service of the Danish Church. This is not to be derived from Scripture but is independent of it and has an authority which takes precedence of it. His view here is of such importance that it may be best to give it in his own words.

"In my earlier period I assumed, in common with the scholars of the past, that the best way to prove the genuinely Christian character of the faith we profess in baptism was by means of Holy Scripture and the written history of the Christian Church, and that one could then go on to prove the truth of Christianity and the divine origin of the Bible from the remarkable history of the Church and our own experience within it. But I have entirely changed my mind. [He is referring here to a work which he had projected and even commenced, in two parts. The first was to set out the content of the Christian faith and the second to marshal the evidences for its truth]. It came to me in a flash that if we appeal to the Bible and other ancient books as witnesses to the genuinely Christian character of the faith of our fathers—a faith which has been challenged in our day and even by many who call themselves Christian bishops, pastors, and professors—we are appealing to something which we ourselves do not really know and which uneducated Christians, in so far as they know it, can only read in a translation. It

seems difficult to know what to do here, yet it is easy after all, as soon as we remember that the profession of faith at baptism is a quite sufficient witness to what ought to be believed by all who wish to be Christians, so that whoever denies this faith or rejects even the least part of it, acknowledged as it is not only by Lutherans but by Catholics as well, is evidently no Christian—unless, to be sure, the Christian Church was falsified far back in the earliest days of the Church, and he who wishes to assert that should be prepared to prove it.
"This confession of faith teaches us how we as Christians are to understand Scripture, and it teaches us at the same time to distinguish between the Christian faith which we have in common with all who were Christians before us or will be such after us and our own knowledge. If we hold fast to the word of faith, which is the living voice of the Spirit, explaining and interpreting the letter of Scripture thereby, we shall then be able with success to defend the faith against its enemies and to strengthen it among the doubting. For so long as we try to derive the faith from Scripture, we shall be arguing till the Day of Judgement with our enemies about what the Christian faith is that we are to defend; so long also will the Christian community remain in uncertainty, vexed by all those innumerable and in part interminable doubts which arise when one is reading an ancient book which has gone through many hands and which has so many-sided, so profound, and therefore often necessarily so obscure a content as the Bible has."

If we analyse this passage, we can detect in it at least four trains of thought. In the first place, Grundtvig is concerned to make a first-hand religion possible for the common man. He cannot endure to think that the simple believer must remain always in tutelage to the scholar. In the second place, he wants to stress the universal elements in Christianity as opposed to the confessional expressions of it: the Creed is common ground to Catholic and Protestant, Lutheran and Reformed: it nourished the spiritual life of our fathers and we hand it on to our children. Thirdly, there is the contrast between old and new: the Bible is an ancient book and therefore in some respects remote from us; we need to have something which can enter more fully into our life to-day than a book written long ago in what are now dead languages. Finally, Grundtvig opposed the living word spoken in the Church to the letter of Scripture.

Here we are introduced to one of the most important of his thoughts, and one which was equally influential on the territory of education, as the next chapter will show. It is curious that he who was a voracious reader of books and an unwearied writer of them, a man of the study rather than of the open air or the city street, should have expressed so often such an abhorrence of books! But to him the word has metaphysical significance as

> 'the mark of the human in distinction from the animal, the expression of our wonderful inner life, the evidence of our likeness to God. He who was the complete image of God was therefore called also the Word of God. But the word is always spoken, the sole invisible expression of the invisible Spirit. What is written, on the other hand, is not nature but an artificial product; not word properly so called but shadow and grave of the word. Every book is in itself a dead thing; the life we discern as we read is not in the book but in us: we ourselves add what makes all the difference. No book can confer life, not even the Bible. The Christian community is no mere reading-club; it is a fellowship of faith begotten and preserved through the spoken word as this goes down from generation to generation.'

§

The question may be asked: How did Grundtvig arrive at this conclusion? He has given us two answers. According to the one account, he reached it by a sudden inspiration which came to him as the result of prayer and the reading of Irenaeus. According to the other, it was the climax, slowly reached, of just that train of thought which has been set out above—the necessity for some authority which will be accessible to the ordinary Christian without the mediation of professional scholars. In his criticism of the 'incomparable discovery' Kierkegaard points out that Grundtvig had been anticipated in this by Lessing, and recent research has shown that views remarkably similar were in fact taught in his lectures by the professor of church history at Copenhagen under whom he studied theology. We can easily suppose that he was subconsciously prepared for what came to him at the time with the force of an inspiration. Certainly his debt to Irenaeus was considerable and was acknowledged to be such, for it was from this father that he learned to regard the Creed as of apostolic authority.

As such it was earlier than the New Testament and is therefore independent of it. It has been transmitted from believer to believer down the centuries and thus links up the Church of a later day with its very earliest times. It can therefore be regarded with confidence as the authoritative expression of what a Christian should believe—unless, as was said above, the Church has in fact lived for centuries in grave error and this would be so serious a position to maintain that he who would do so must produce good reasons for it. In plain fact, therefore, Grundtvig holds to the infallibility of the Church, at least as regards fundamentals. Is not this Catholicism rather than Lutheranism? Yes and no. Yes, inasmuch as it sets so high a value on the tradition of the Church, actually rating it above Scripture. No, because the community as such and not its clergy are the custodians of this tradition, which is appealed to precisely in order to dispense with such tutelage of the laity by the priesthood as is indispensable on the Roman system. But what are we to say of the contention that the onus of proof lies with those who would question the authority of the Church and its formula? In reality that is the desperate attempt of a man who has no arguments left to silence his opponents. We can get nowhere once it is admitted that an assertion can be thrown out and those who do not accept it required to disprove it! In point of fact, the Creed raises as many critical difficulties as the Bible: it too is an ancient document which has come down to us in written form, indeed in more than one written form. Which of these is to be taken as apostolic? Does it in fact go back to the apostles at all? Once that question is asked, it is clear that there is as little certainty here as there was elsewhere. Certainty is only to be found by blind faith somewhere, and if one is prepared to believe blindly, there is no need to leave the Bible for the Church. As Kierkegaard rightly maintained, there is need for a new 'introductory discipline' which will deal with all these questions before we can build our faith on what is offered to us so confidently.

Various attempts were made, after a fashion, to meet this difficulty. Lindberg, one of Grundtvig's followers, argued that whereas the Bible belongs to the past and so needs all sorts of demonstrations, the Church is a present reality and as such can dispense with them. It is there for all to see. But, as Kierkegaard points out, there is an enormous assumption in this naïve presentation of the case: it is assumed that this church which is before our eyes is in unbroken continuity with the Church of the apostles, a claim which may or may not be valid, but which certainly is open to historical investigation.

Grundtvig himself went to work more boldly and

asserted that the Creed derived from Jesus himself. That there is no sign of this in the New Testament only serves to enhance its value: it is the living word *par excellence*, which was spoken by the Lord and thereafter transmitted orally. The coping-stone was added to this theological structure by Kierkegaard's brother, who placed the communication of the Creed to the apostles in the forty days after the Resurrection—an empty period into which one can put what one likes, without any possibility of being refuted.

§

It is easy to criticize this elevation of an ancient creed into the place from which an ancient book had just been removed. Grundtvig's whole position is highly vulnerable, nevertheless there is that in it which refuses to yield to any criticism: otherwise, it would not have influenced Danish church life as it did. Certainly in all this he was giving expression to no mere private theory, but rather to one of the deepest spiritual needs of the time. All over Western Europe a reaction had set in against the individualism of the Age of Reason and its want of understanding for the social groupings in which the individual is embedded, as well as for the traditions out of which he emerges and by which he is sustained. Hence the cult of the middle ages in the literature of the time, the Catholic revival in France at the Restoration, and the idealization of humanity in the political thinking of Mazzini. Grundtvig, it must be remembered, was a contemporary of Pusey and Newman: he also was a high-churchman, though, as we have seen, he had little understanding for the Oxford Movement. The idea of the Church was invading even the social philosophy of the time, as we can see, for example, in Saint-Simon and Comte. A craving for fellowship was abroad, the longing to share in a common life which binds together past, present, and future. Grundtvig was therefore no solitary phenomenon and no specifically Danish one, but a child of his time.

We have already dealt in passing with the charge of Catholicism. Certainly he wanted a church as the bearer of salvation by its rites of baptism and the Lord's Supper, but a people's church, not a church of the clergy. Yet at times he used language which suggested a grave departure from the Protestant position, as when he translated the great battle-hymn of the Reformation in a form which suggested that the Church rather than God was the stronghold in which faith takes refuge, or in another of his hymns makes the prodigal son return to the bosom of Mother Church. This was a consequence of his peculiar type of individualism, for which the free personality develops in unity with the nation to which it belongs or, in this case, as a member of the Church.

We might say that what Grundtvig was trying to express was that Christianity is not a sacred book, which is of necessity closed and therefore dated in the past, but a continuous life in fellowship which goes down the ages and in which we ourselves are called upon to take part. It is a spiritual movement which is not to be arrested at any point in time, as though it were complete then and nothing could follow except the exact reproduction of what has been so far achieved. It is a heritage into which we enter, a hope by which we are sustained, a task which is assigned to us and a blessing which we are privileged to hand on to our children. The essence of Christianity does not lie in any fixed body of doctrine but in the unity which is somehow present in all the diverse forms it has assumed in the course of the centuries, the unity which is so rich that it brings forth these forms out of its own fulness and still has more to be revealed.

Of course, Christianity cannot be identified simply with a process of change; there must be some norm which enables us to decide which, out of the countless phenomena which have borne the Christian name, are entitled to it and which are not. Is the veneration of saints legitimate? Is the doctrine of justification by faith the heart of the Gospel or a gross perversion of it? Have the 'German Christians' a place in the continuity of the Church's teaching? An authority there must be somewhere and Grundtvig finds it in what he accepts—to be sure, on quite insufficient evidence—to be a statement of Christianity as it was in its classical period, when the influence of the Master upon his disciples was still fresh and he was able to express his mind directly to them. Had the Apostles' Creed been what he imagined it to be, the account which Jesus himself gave of his life's purpose, it might well have served as the norm for which he was seeking. We should then have had the simple and satisfying position that the Christian attaches himself in each generation to the historic community with its shared life, while the community preserves in the baptismal confession the criterion which enables even the least equipped to distinguish between where it is true to its mission and where it departs from it.

Of course, it is by no means as easy as that. Christianity lives both by the original impulse out of which it arose and the highly diversified historical development of that impulse. These, if we like to use the term, are its two authorities, neither of which can be dispensed with and which it is not always easy to reconcile; but it must be stated clearly that in neither case can infallibility be claimed. If we wish to know whether some idea or practice is genuinely Christian we may ask either whether it is acceptable to the common Christian mind, in so far as that can be ascertained, or whether it harmonizes with the picture of Christ preserved for us in the earliest parts of the New Testament, in so far as they can be reconstructed by historical enquiry. We shall do well, however, to ask both questions, and even then the answer will be one of spiritual discernment, not a logical inference from accepted premisses.

§

The high-church theology of Grundtvig turned, of course, not only on the Creed but also on the sacraments. Indeed, the Creed was for him indissolubly associated with the rite of baptism as that by which the individual enters into the fellowship of the Christian society. He speaks of baptism as a covenant and regards it as an institution of the Lord. Here he is on the weakest possible ground, since the only text to which he can appeal is Matthew xxviii, 19, and the mention of the trinitarian formula shows that this cannot go back to Jesus. Further, he actually makes the renunciation of 'the devil and all his works' an integral part of the rite along with the profession of faith. What he does is in fact to invest with dominical authority the practice, in this respect, of Danish Lutheranism!

At the same time, this emphasis on baptism is in the interest of Grundtvig's democratic and universalistic tendencies alike. The Christian life begins, not with a doctrine, but with an action which can be appreciated by the simplest: moreover, it widens the frontiers of the Church so that it can take in those who stand outside the particular communion to which one belongs oneself. 'He who acknowledges the faith and submits himself to the basic Christian institutions of the Church as the Lord's command and leads a Christian life, let him be as peculiar, as childish, or as cryptic as he wishes, let him be Roman Catholic or Reformed, I regard him as a fellow-Christian and a member of the one Christian Church, and I leave it to the God who knows the hearts of his children to judge how far he really is what he seems to be.' In comparison with baptism, only a secondary place is assigned to the Lord's Supper.

To what extent does Grundtvig in this depart from his

Lutheran heritage? We now know that the rediscovery of the sacraments in the last century was not a repudiation of the Reformers, but a return to them. Infrequent communion is a survival of the awe with which the altar was surrounded, in medieval Catholicism, thanks to the dogma of transubstantiation. Calvin wished to have the sacrament weekly in Geneva but was unable to carry his point against the civic authorities. But in some important respects Grundtvig seems to depart from the Protestant tradition. He stresses baptism rather than the supper, whereas the Reformation might be regarded, from one point of view, as an effort to substitute the congregational communion service for the sacrifice of the Mass. He can even declare in one of his hymns—surely without meaning fully what he said—that 'only in baptism and the cup does the Lord speak to us.' Again, the 'living word' in the strict sense of that term is not the sermon, but the Creed and the words of institution which accompany and validate the sacramental observance. No doubt, few men have had a stronger sense of the power of the spoken word as personal communication, the utterance of faith which kindles faith; no doubt also the living word has come to mean just this for his followers, whether he who speaks it is preacher or lecturer. Nevertheless, this broader conception belongs rather to his practice and his educational theories than to his specifically theological point of view.

§

So Grundtvig sought to bring to his people a new sense of the significance of the Church for the Christian life. He wanted to make the Church the centre of the community in the villages of Denmark, the home of a free and manly piety, reinforced by the consciousness of solidarity with the living and the dead and of a continuity which reached back to the Lord himself and his apostles. To do this he made use also of the Christian year and of the hymns by which these are celebrated annually. He wanted a singing church rather than a church of sermon-tasters, for he saw that the Christian education of many members of a country congregation will come more effectively through the hymn-book than through any other medium. Himself one of Denmark's greatest poets, he put his lyrical genius at the service of the Church; altogether, some 1,500 hymns came from his pen.

Not all of these were original, of course: he drew without hesitation on his predecessors and on the hymnody of other countries for his material. His translations, however, were usually recastings of that material in a form which accorded with his own genius. More than most western Christians, he was able to enter sympathetically into the Orthodox message of the transfiguration of nature by Christ: his antithesis, it will be remembered, was that of life and death. 'As he had bestowed on Irenaeus such high praise, so he was never able quite to tear himself away from the third century in which that father lived, still using Greek as his medium, the heroic age of the struggling community, not yet subservient to the state nor petrified into a church, when it still lived by the apostolic traditions and was at home in the ancient culture.' But he utilized also Latin, German, and English originals to enrich the treasury of the Danish Church.

These hymns and those which he added to them from his own composition were grouped around the great Christian festivals and were designed to foster in the common people love of the Church and its services, the day of rest and the bells inviting to worship. Christmas and Easter have therefore a place of first importance, but in connection with the latter it is noticeable that Grundtvig prefers to speak of the Resurrection rather than the Passion. As we have already seen, even in suffering Christ is for him the all-conquering hero. As Lehmann has said of him: 'He planted the lilies of the resurrection in the place where the cross of pain had stood, let the flowers of life grow over and cover the grave.'

But Grundtvig is pre-eminently the poet of Whitsuntide and the Holy Spirit. Here we have to remember that spring comes later in Denmark than with ourselves and so synchronizes with Whitsuntide rather than with Easter. And Grundtvig was naturally qualified to appreciate and to sing of the festival of the Spirit, the giver of life, freedom, and creativity, 'Had Kierkegaard decided the future of the Church, there would have been little place in it for the Holy Spirit. Indeed it has been disputed whether he ever so much as mentioned him. He saw God only as revealed through the Son, Grundtvig more and more as revealed through the Spirit.' Therefore while the one demanded the sacrifice of reason to an incredible dogma of the Incarnation, the other set men free by the proclamation of God as willing life and life to the uttermost. His ideal was the free personality as the vehicle of the Spirit, life communicating life to others. And his mission was that of Ezekiel, to bid the winds of God blow upon his people, that where dry bones lay in the valley to-day, to-morrow an army of the living God might stand.

§

How far did he accomplish this? He set the Church again in the hearts of his people and he diffused through the national life something of the Christian faith and the Christian ethic. He did not, however, make of them a nation of church-goers: in Denmark, as elsewhere, the majority of the people are only nominally attached to the Church, using it for baptisms, marriages, and funerals. Nevertheless, he has left a deep impression upon the life of his people, so that a Dane can say of him that 'his influence can be detected to this day in almost every area of the national life and there are few persons in Denmark who are not to some extent affected by his work.' But in order to understand how this has come about, we must pass on from 'the living word' in the Church to the 'living word' in the school. True to his own contention that civil society needs the Church to free it and the school to train it, Grundtvig saw in a new type of education the best means to the permanent renewal of the life of his people.

7

Education for Life

NATURALLY enough, Grundtvig's educational theories were the outcome of his own experience. They were a eulogy of flight by a bird escaped from its cage. He was never able to forget the two years spent at Aarhaus in the grammar school—the endless memorizings, the dull grind at a dead language, and the strait-jacket of the examination system. Books, books—were there no other sources of wisdom than these? Did one learn a language, then, for the sake of its grammar and not for the new window opening out upon life that one might hope to find in its literature? And why the Latin language, with its pedantry and legalism, all so alien to the free spirit of the northern peoples? When he went on to the university, he began to ask himself how many of his fellow-students were at home among the traditions of their own people or loved their mother tongue as old Malene and his mother loved it.

Apart from its defective methods, two evils flowed from the system to which he had been subjected as a youth. In the first place, it created an educated caste, whose members were cut off from the life of their people and had no sympathy with their fellows. The human person was sacrificed to the career he proposed to take up; he was forced into the shape required to enable him to fit neatly into one of those 'openings' which society had ready to offer to conformists. But was there no purpose in education beyond the production of a certain number of professional men and officials? Why should these men, so self-satisfied and self-important, go on then to refuse to the peasant the key into the realm of culture while they themselves could make so little use of it? So our own educational system has been criticized on the ground that it has no objective except the employment of teachers to make more teachers!

In the second place, those who had come under the influence of grammar school and university seemed to Grundtvig to have acquired nothing of more value than a certain amount of antiquarian lumber and to have lost something precious—vitality. The critical faculty was developed at the expense of the creative powers; men came out of such a training stocked with the opinions of other people but incapable of any of their own, 'immeasurably rich in ideas, but great beggars in reality.'

It became therefore an urgent matter with him to bring into existence a wholly different type of education, one which would develop life as the other tended towards death. This would reach the mass of the people and would break altogether with the formal methods of the past. Even before Grundtvig had gone over to the democratic cause in politics, he saw that such steps in that direction as the appointment in 1834 of people's advisory councils called for appropriate training to be given to those who might soon be admitted to a share in power. The passage from absolutism to liberty could only be made with success if the individual, whatever his social status, had the type of character which would enable him to use his freedom for the common good.

One of the most original, and perhaps in the long run the most valuable, of Grundtvig's suggestions was that this new type of education should be given at the age of eighteen. He did not neglect entirely the earlier period, for had he not been at one time a private tutor and at another a master in a Copenhagen secondary school? He wanted the principle of freedom to be recognized from the outset, the development of the child's personality replacing the imposition upon him of an approved pattern of conduct. As for the secondary school, he was convinced that the time spent there was longer than necessary for most of those who attended: some lads, no doubt, were naturally fitted for an academic career, but the majority would do far better to leave at fourteen and spend some time in the open air in touch with nature and in the home of some honest craftsman, learning his trade. During those years the wisest of all teachers, life itself, would be busy with its instruction; the lad would become aware of life's problems and his own responsibilities; he would thus develop the desire to learn more in order to fit himself for manhood and citizenship. When the age of eighteen came, with his enthusiasms roused and questionings astir in his mind, let him come to a school which will give him what he needs—a spiritual view of life, an attachment to his fellows and his country, and a new understanding of his daily work as the means of serving them. That would be the function of the Folk High-School. The type of education fostered there would be different from the traditional one, both in content and in method.

§

As regards content, the subject which seemed to Grundtvig of supreme importance was history. Not of course as a mass of facts and dates to be memorized, but as a tradition of valour and achievement from which we can derive inspiration for our present tasks. It enables a man to find his place in his own nation and in the race, to know the heritage into which he has entered and to discern the work of God in which he is called to take a share. He draws upon a larger experience than his own, widens his sympathies, and comes to an understanding of human nature in himself and in his fellows. All this, of course, is in line with the romantic interpretation of history; but events have shown us how deplorable is the position of the man who is no longer in touch with any sound tradition, how unhappy he becomes in himself and what a menace he may be to his society. Personal freedom seems in fact to be best developed where one is in living touch with a community in the present and the past to whose tradition one gives an individual expression.

In the second place Grundtvig put the Danish language and literature. By the latter he meant particularly the legends of the country's heroic past, but room was to be found also for modern prophets and seers, and for poets whose work might be read aloud. He believed—and who shall say that he was wrong?—that there is a close relation between what we may call the genius of a people and the language in which it expresses itself; the mother teaching her children to speak gives them, all unconsciously, a *Weltanschauung* and a standard of values. He wanted no intellectual cosmopolitans, but Danes who were proud to be such and who respected other countries just because they had learned to give such love to their own. And any training to take part in public life must include the mastery of one's mother tongue: anyone who has worked in adult education in our own country knows how many men of acute intellect are frustrated by the lack of ability to express themselves with ease. To assist in this, Grundtvig planned to let conversation do what is otherwise sought by formal instruction in grammar and composition.

In the third place, singing was one of the essentials of this education for life. He saw the power of community singing to weld the members of a group together even while it enkindles the enthusiasm of the individual. He wanted in particular to revive those songs which belonged to the past of his people and were still freighted with history; alongside of these, he set some of his own compositions which would express just that vitality, that love of freedom, and that responsibility of the part for the whole which he was concerned to inculcate. In the folk high-schools of to-day singing plays a part of great importance and sometimes a lecture will be rounded off with a song which serves to lodge more securely in the minds of the listeners the ideals which have been commended to them.

Finally, mention must be made of a fourth and most comprehensive subject, the study, we may call it, of contemporary conditions in Denmark. Here instruction would be given best by one who had travelled widely and could speak of what he had seen in various parts of the country: he could thus leave with his hearers a vivid impression of what the nation most needed and what one part of it could teach another. But more than instruction was necessary, and Grundtvig wished the students to keep in touch with the busy life of the society from which they had withdrawn for a while only that they might serve it more adequately on their return. He suggested therefore that a farm in the neighbourhood might be attached to the high-school and that the students might have access to workshops. 'It would be of inestimable benefit for the young people both to see the future craft of each one of them practised in masterly fashion, and to have before their eyes the living variety to which their wise teachers would constantly direct their attention.' While Grundtvig wished these schools to give a general preparation for life and adult responsibility rather than vocational training as such, he wanted those who had benefited by this to be willing to return to work on the farm: there must be no such separation of culture from one's daily calling as has been the vice of too many educational systems.

§

In all this, of course, he is not planning the curriculum of a new type of school so much as throwing out ideas on which he hopes that others will act. And the question of method is of equal importance with that of the subjects to be taught. Emphasis was laid, here also, on 'the living word.' Not formal instruction, but the communication of personal life, was what he desired. As a necessary preliminary to that, there must be the maximum amount of freedom for teacher and student alike. Education must be voluntary, given because it is sought and therefore all the more effective. Equally, the principal of the school must not work to a syllabus imposed on him by some outside authority but must draw up the time-table so as best to meet the needs of his students and at the same time as best accords with his own peculiar equipment and experience. Especially in religion was Grundtvig opposed to any form of compulsion and the result is that, while a large proportion of the heads of folk high-schools to-day are men with a theological training, the religious element in the schools is present more as something which pervades its whole life than as one subject among others.

The living word would, under these conditions, have free play both in lecture and in conversation. Coming at an age in which they were already aware of the problems of life, the students would be eager to converse with others and in particular with persons of a riper experience than their own. Hence time must be allowed for conversation and discussion and the teacher must be prepared to adapt the curriculum to the needs of individuals. The teaching itself must have something about it of the prophetic character, so as to serve the awakening and development of personality by interpreting the common life in the midst of which the individual is set. Something of what this means we can learn from the closing paragraph of Peter Manniche's account of a day in a modern school of this type:

> 'The old pupil, looking back over his stay at the high-school, may ask himself what it was that, despite all

differences of temperament and outlook, created the life of fellowship: and he discovers that it was the spirit that lived in the song, the spirit that gleamed forth every time the spoken word was really the *living word*. The word was living when the speaker became impersonal, when he seemed to disappear as a teacher, and, in all humility, remained only the instrument and messenger of the eternal spirit, the spirit carrying all development, revealing itself in changing circumstances and in the lives of individuals, the spirit which is the deepest reality, which is the revealer of God.'

One of Grundtvig's friends has summed up for us the educational ideal of his master as follows: 'The spirit is power; the spirit works through the word; the spirit works only in freedom.' And one of the most active workers in the earlier days of the folk high-school movement has given us a classic statement of its aims and methods in a protest which he lodged against the attempt to impose upon them a formal examination:

'This institution certainly does not underestimate the importance of specialist knowledge and the development of the intellect to keenness and clearness; but its aim is essentially educational; the development of the feelings and the will has for it more importance than the exercise of the memory and the reason. It seeks to do in the national and educational sphere what the Church does in the sphere of religion. Therefore it must lay the chief stress on what is living, stimulating, vivid; and the hour in which it has succeeded in arousing a feeling for the high and noble things of human life and giving a stimulus to active work for their advancement has a greater significance for the folk high-school than those hours in which new items of knowledge are added to those already possessed. . . . Our learning is for life and not for the school. We wish our students to leave us with the desire to devote themselves to the tasks of life and to use with understanding the means which life offers.'

§

This book is concerned with Grundtvig himself and his work, and only quite secondarily with the influences which have continued to flow from him after his death. Nevertheless, this brief account of his ideas in the realm of education needs to be supplemented by some reference to what has been done to give reality to them, both in Denmark and in other countries. But first it must be pointed out that the actual development has taken another course than the one which he himself intended for it. Enjoying as he did royal patronage, it was natural that he should seek to enlist the king on his side and should think in terms of the transformation of the existing academy at Soro into a high-school after his own heart. It seemed at one time quite possible that this might be done, but after the death of Christian VIII in 1848 and the transition from absolutism to constitutional monarchy, the project was dropped. Grundtvig did not, however, abandon his dream of a great Scandinavian university in which the scholars of the North would be united, and their peoples through them. He wanted this to replace the existing national institutions and to provide at a higher level the same education for life as the mass of the people might find in the folk high-schools. He envisaged it as a great corporate enterprise of study, research, and teaching in which freedom would rule and in which students and teachers would be bound together as in a fraternity. Perhaps some recollections of his stay at Trinity College, Cambridge, have entered into this plan, but the model to which he professes to have worked is that of ancient Athens when conversation and discussion were the means by which the wisdom of life was communicated.

Mention has already been made of the school at Rodding, founded as part of the cultural resistance to German advance in Schleswig: with the transfer of this area to Germany, the school was moved across the border and re-established at Askov, where it became perhaps the most successful of all the institutions which Grundtvig inspired. The name most closely associated with it is that of Ludwig Schroeder, under whose principalship the change of situation was made. To his duties as teacher he added those of a member of Parliament and he made it his aim to weld together the cultural training given in the school with the requirements of practical life on the farm and in the town. He therefore welcomed the co-operation of la Cour, who was able to introduce into the curriculum the teaching of science without any sacrifice of the high-school spirit, while he himself was responsible for a model farm in the neighbourhood. He was eager in every way to link up the school with the people of the district and therefore from time to time arranged public lectures for their benefit, while in the autumn he organized short periods of instruction to occupy the farmers' leisure once the harvest had been gathered in. It is to-day a school of distinctly higher grade than most of the others, and many of those who come to it have taken a first course elsewhere and are now going on to be trained as teachers themselves in other institutions.

With the success of the new educational venture in the years of national awakening after the defeat of 1864, the idea was taken up by others. The revivalist movement known in Denmark as the Inner Mission opened its own schools, in which the religious purpose was more in evidence than in those which derived from Grundtvig. The Danish Baptists have a school of their own. Others have been founded for political objectives. But more important are the agricultural schools which have arisen naturally by specializing in that technical training which the folk high-schools did not give, but whose value they recognized. The latest figures available show that just before the war there were twenty such colleges in Denmark with an enrolment of more than 2,000 students. 'It may be said that about 20 per cent. of the young men on the land participate in a course at an agricultural college at some time of their unmarried life. A part of these students will have taken a course at a folk high-school before they enter an agricultural college. Between one-third and one-half of all those farmers who have a holding of their own have been either to a folk high-school or to an agricultural school or to both.'

What is the organization of a typical folk high-school? It is an embodiment of the ideal of freedom and as such is dependent on voluntary support. The sums required for the first schools were raised by public subscription and Kold's venture was made on so small a capital sum that the story goes that when he cleared away the tumble-down farm which he had bought to make way for a new building, he had to remove the nails from the timber, hammer them straight, and use them again. Some schools are owned by the principal, others by a group of individuals who have at heart the ideals which it exists to serve. Attendance, of course, is quite voluntary and every student is expected to contribute something towards the expense of his course. The state has long since recognized the value of such work and makes regular grants in aid of it. According to the latest legislation before the war, the state made a grant equal to 50 per cent. of the salaries of the teachers plus 20 per cent. of that of the principal, 10 per cent. of the annual expenses on the buildings, and 35 per cent. of the expenditure on materials required for the course. In addition state scholarships were available for attendance at recognized schools.

Under this system, the state has the right of inspection to ensure that certain standards are maintained, but it does not examine and it leaves the curriculum to the principal. The normal course is one of five months in the winter, which may be supplemented by attendance at a shorter one in the summer. Women's courses are of somewhat shorter duration. Since the students are all eager to learn, the fullest possible use is made of the time available, so that what would appear to the outsider as a heavily-loaded time-table has sometimes to be supplemented to meet the requests of individual pupils with special interests.

At the outbreak of the war, there were fifty-seven folk high-schools in Denmark with 5,800 students, the number being composed of men and women practically equally. It was only in accordance with their traditions that some of them should be in the forefront of the resistance movement during the days of German occupation and two at least were closed. The majority however were allowed to continue and are to-day in good heart to maintain their work.

§

Though the folk high-school began in Denmark it had a mission from the outset to all the Scandinavian peoples and it was not long before it was accepted among them all. Especially in Finland did it render valuable service as a means of maintaining the national culture and the spirit of liberty even under the tsarist régime. In Sweden during the last ten years the movement has gone forward by leaps and bounds, though state control and support have been extended to it in a greater measure than in Denmark. From time to time conferences are held for teachers and students from all the Scandinavian countries and in addition two schools for all the northern peoples have been founded, one in Frederiksborg and the other at Geneva. In these, of course, the teaching of languages occupies a prominent place in the curriculum.

Other countries too have followed the Danish example. In England, Fircroft Adult School was opened in Birmingham in 1908, with Tom Bryan at its head. Wales has had its Coleg Harlech since 1927, and the last twenty years have seen further extensions in the way of residential provision for adult education in Great Britain. The Workers' Educational Association has organized each year several summer schools, attended often by workers who gave up for the purpose part or the whole of their annual holiday, while during the years of economic depression courses of a week or a fortnight were provided for unemployed workers. Anyone who has attended such schools can bear witness at once to their heartening influence on those who attended them and on the grave problem which they could raise but could not solve, that of the adjustment of the unemployed man to the social conditions to which he was compelled to return at the end.

On the Continent the folk high-school was introduced after 1918 into Germany as a means of national renewal, though necessarily in a manner adapted to the needs of an urban population. China and Japan have learned from the same source, and Peter Manniche in 1934 toured the Far East to commend to social workers there what had been so powerful for good in his own country.

His name is associated with one of the boldest ventures in the history of the movement, the establishment at Elsinore of the International People's College as the direct outcome of the war of 1914–1918. Even during the war, money was contributed for a project which was to serve the reconciliation of the peoples once the struggle was over, and the buildings were opened for use in 1921. The first batch of students numbered twenty-four, and was made up as follows: 2 Americans, 5 from the United Kingdom, 5

Germans, 3 Austrians, and the rest Danes. The main difficulty was not so much that of language—manual work, singing, and language classes all helped to solve that problem—but the widely divergent attitudes of the various nationalities. The Germans, for example, wanted formal instruction by a teacher who was an authority on his subject, while the British preferred the techniques of the study circle and the discussion group. The school soon attracted students from other nationalities and the annual summer school in particular became a most popular event. During the war the building was occupied by the Germans but it was not long before the principal was over in this country to announce the resumption of his work and to recruit students.

§

If we ask what contribution the folk high-schools have made to the life of Denmark, the answer is that they have had both a general vitalizing effect and an influence upon particular classes and for the solution of particular problems. Their part in making possible the recovery of the nation after the defeat at the hands of Germany and in enabling it to regain inwardly what it had lost outwardly, has perhaps been sufficiently stressed. While the schools as such were definitely non-political in character, it was inevitable that they should send many members to Parliament and should contribute leaders to the Peasants' Party and even ministers to the cabinet. Equally important is the part which men trained in these schools have played in building up the Danish system of co-operation in agriculture. In the first half of last century the basis of Danish economy was corn-growing and a variety of circumstances combined to make this exceptionally profitable. With the abolition of the Corn Laws the English market was opened to the Danish exporter, the discovery of gold in western America led to a rise in prices, and finally the democratic reforms of 1848 removed the last restrictions upon the freedom and initiative of the farmer. All this, however, was rudely interrupted by the development of vast grain-growing areas in the United States, Canada, Argentina and Siberia. It was impossible to face competition from these sources. Tariffs might have been resorted to, but the Danish farmers possessed a resilience of mind which enabled them not merely to resist this threat to their prosperity, but even to pluck advantage from it. They changed over to dairy-farming and utilized the cheap grain available from overseas for feeding their live-stock. At the same time co-operation was organized so as to enable the new industry to win and secure its place in the world-market. By this means Denmark has been able to combine the advantages of large-scale organization with those of the small-holding in which the farmer and his family are personally interested in the success of the enterprise. While it cannot be claimed that the co-operative societies which cover the country to-day are the direct outcome of the folk high-schools and their cultural training, it is certain that the latter gave to the people the qualities and the leadership which enabled them to meet and overcome this crisis.

All this means, however, that the schools are related rather to the past than to the present. They arose in a society of farmers and small-scale enterprise and Grundtvig seems to have supposed that this social pattern would continue to be the dominant one in the country. He was not prepared either for the advances in science or for the industrialization of the country which present together new problems to all educational systems. The curriculum which he sketched was derived largely from the romantic movement and the impulses it gave; it is impossible to-day to shut one's eyes to the impact of science on society and the realism which it has brought with it. Hence the instruction given now has to be less informal than that with which, say, Kold could be content, and a place has to be found for the study of science and of foreign languages. Here, however, the historical method can still be employed. Indeed, the teaching of science gains greatly by its employment, for the student then is not merely given a certain number of results to get by heart but is initiated into an enterprise. It was perhaps only to be expected that with the turn of the century signs should appear that new sources of enthusiasm and energy needed to be found; fortunately the folk high-school movement is still served by a number of able young men who can be trusted to meet the new situation with courage.

The main problem which confronts them is that of applying to an urban population methods which worked so successfully in rural areas. Although so large a part of his life was spent in the capital, Grundtvig did not leave on it anything like the impression which he left on the countryside. The folk high-school idea, too, was slow to take root among the industrial proletariat. Conditions, of course, were by no means favourable, since the city worker cannot leave his machine for five months as, with some domestic arrangement, the farmer's son or daughter is able to leave the holding. Johan Borup made the attempt to reach the city population, beginning with courses of lectures, both during the day and after working-hours in the evening. It was thus something like what we in this country used to know as a "mechanics' institute." A parallel movement came from some of the social-democratic leaders who in 1924 set up a Workers' Educational Association to foster all forms of adult education; before long it was in receipt of state grants in aid of its work. It now owns two folk high-schools, at Esbjerg and Roskilde respectively: each can receive over 100 students for its main course in the winter and provides also a shorter course in the summer. These two schools were closed by the Germans during their occupation of the country, but opened again on liberation. It is clear that considerable adaptation is needed before the work of such schools can be made suitable to an industrial population, but it is even more clear that the need is now even greater among the city workers than in the country districts. Perhaps the very success of the movement in the rural areas made it difficult for it to adapt itself in Denmark to a new constituency, and it is probable that British experience of the organization of adult education on a voluntary basis has more to offer than anything that has yet been done in Denmark. This book is written while it is still uncertain how adult education will develop among us under the new Education Act, but there are indications that the residential college may come into its own before long. The proposal for the establishment of county colleges may also provide an opportunity for just that education for life on which Grundtvig laid such stress. In these institutions it should be possible to give a more adequate preparation for the duties of citizenship and at the same time to stimulate thought on the ultimate questions which lie behind all our social and personal problems. That we need a national renewal in the spiritual sphere is surely evident to all, and there is not a little which we can learn from that bold conception of education which Grundtvig gave to his time and which has been acted on with such great success in his country.

§

In what has been said so far, no reference has been made to Grundtvig's indebtedness to others. While what he gave to his time was specifically his own and fired by his personality, we cannot doubt that he had himself learned from others, especially from Rousseau and Fichte. Lehmann, to be sure, appears gravely to overestimate the influence of the former upon him. Nevertheless, the idea that the self can only develop in freedom and that it can be trusted so to develop, is common to both the Dane and the Swiss. And Rousseau too lays emphasis upon the necessity of introducing the student to what is best in his national culture rather than instilling in him a vague cosmopolitanism. But we do not know that Grundtvig had any direct knowledge of his predecessor's work and must be content to suppose that certain ideas were in the air at the time and reached him so.

With Fichte the case is different, as we have evidence that Grundtvig was deeply indebted to him and that his moral earnestness left upon him an abiding impression. It must be remembered that the German advocated education as a means of spiritual renewal and as a weapon of resistance to the French conqueror. He too idealized the past and wished his hearers to take pride in their ancestry as an antidote to the disappointments and disheartenments of their own day. He hoped for the transformation of the German people in a single generation by a type of education which would be national, ethical, and practical. Nor could we desire a better illustration of the 'living word' than in those famous *Addresses to the German Nation* by which he rallied his people for the coming struggle, even while he urged them to wage it with the weapons of the spirit.

What came of Fichte's burning words was, however, something very different in the end from the legacy which Grundtvig has left to posterity. If the former has been accepted as one of the forerunners of National-Socialism, the latter deserves to be remembered as a prophet who could summon his people to such a love of country as would make them at the same time the leaders in international co-operation they have become. It is his merit to have baptized into Christ so much that elsewhere has tended to materialism or an arrogant, aggressive nationalism. He has shown, by contrast with his great contemporary and critic

Kierkegaard, that the new world of democracy and social endeavour, national solidarity and human rights is not opposed to the Christian faith, but can be enlisted in its service in virtue of the principle which he propounded: 'First a man, and then a Christian.'

www.ingramcontent.com/pod-product-compliance
Lightning Source LLC
Chambersburg PA
CBHW070322100426
42743CB00011B/2527